THE WORST IS YET TO COME:
A POST-CAPITALIST SURVIVAL GUIDE

THE WORST IS YET TO COME: A POST-CAPITALIST SURVIVAL GUIDE

PETER FLEMING

Published by Repeater Books
An imprint of Watkins Media Ltd

Unit 11, Shepperton House
89 Shepperton Road
London
N1 3DF
UK
www.repeaterbooks.com
A Repeater Books paperback original 2019
1

Distributed in the United States by Random House, Inc., New York.

Cover design: Johnny Bull
Typography and typesetting: Frederik Jehle
Typefaces: Meridien LT Std, Archive
Printed and bound in the United Kingdom by TJ International Ltd.

ISBN: 9781912248322
Ebook ISBN: 9781912248339

C O N T E N T S

INTRODUCTION

CIRCLING THE DRAIN

Twenty or so people were waiting outside a grey little apartment. London was cold tonight. It was a "rental viewing" and the agents were late. Even so, given the shortage of accommodation in the city nobody was going anywhere. Including myself. Each of us needed somewhere to live. And fast.

A black BMW pulled up and two suited men stepped out. Mmmm. Men? Both looked about eighteen, more like boys. The British rental market is deregulated and anything goes, so this wasn't surprising.

"Hi guys", the two agents beamed, unlocking the front door as the throng clambered to get out of the cold.

As I entered my worst fears were confirmed. A complete shithole — but one that would still suck up nearly half my monthly salary.

I asked one of the "boys" if the apartment had central heating. "Have no idea," the youngster replied. He was darting from room to room, seemingly without purpose, high on some fashionable amphetamine no doubt.

The other bug-eyed youth demanded to see everyone's passports. He started to photograph them on his phone. The government's new "Hostile Environment" policy concerning illegal immigration meant rental firms had to check everyone's papers.

I pulled out my New Zealand passport and bug-boy froze.

"You better have a valid visa buddy", he hyperventilated. I did as it happened, which he scrutinised with suspicion. "Bit funny looking, isn't it?" he commented. New Zealand passports have a black jacket.

I continued to wander through this glorified cave.

In the bathroom — it hadn't been cleaned since the previous occupants had left, in a hurry apparently — I caught a glimpse of myself in the mirror. The person before me was pale and exhausted. My eyes darkened as I surveyed the damage.

The suited boys were still bullshitting next door. I looked down at my hands. They were tight white balls. Here I was, a forty-four-year-old man, betoken to those two coked-up little shits, begging for an apartment that wouldn't look out of place in *Midnight Cowboy*. Jesus, was I a contemporary manifestation of Ratso Rizzo?

When I arrived in England in 2003, it was so much easier to take the brutality. Conditions were rough back then too, of course. The rent was outlandish and the city resembled a rubbish tip as today; but London's possible overthrow was a unique part of its internal narrative, a radical vitality that reached its darkest corners, breathing life into its wasted infrastructure. The dialectic was in full swing, with cracks of hope opening from nowhere as the city unremittingly turned.

Today the atmosphere was different.

A decade of austerity had drained London of money and existential colour. A new ethno-nationalism was in the air, pitting neighbourhood against neighbourhood, with kid-like bureaucrats subbing as border guards.

The mood reflected a more basic change in the system. An awful balkanisation had crept across the Western world. Espionage was now a legitimate method for managing the populace… and governments loved it. The dialectic proceeded only on its bad-side. London typified that lopsidedness, becoming uninhabitable as the fog descended. And yet its citizens endured like some Beckettian parable.

The grubby sinkhole was black as night and dominated the bathroom. Looking up, I noticed a "Power Shower".

"My god", I whispered.

I'd never seen one of these before arriving in the UK. Now I hated them. They consisted of a modular closet (making them cheaper to install), with plastic buttons (COLD-MEDIUM-HOT) and water pressure that was no stronger than a small child's piddle.

I thought about ripping it off the wall. But the wiring and piping would have made this a challenge. What about scratching the plastic control-unit instead, I asked myself, before realising how pathetic I was.

That awful apartment told me something.

Neoliberal capitalism had probably run its course, spawning progeny it could no longer protect itself from. The constellation of possibilities that once flourished in cities like London had vanished. There were no antibodies left. Capitalism was undoing itself at nearly every turn. A kind of neo-Feudalism was on the march. Perhaps we were witnessing the birth of *post-capitalism* after all, not a clean and better alternative to the system, but (rather paradoxically) a much worse version of it, one that will make the "Trump Years" look like a tiptoe through the tulips.

* * * * * * * * * *

Living in Los Angeles, London, or any other large, aggressive city, you have to put up with a lot of crap. Your physiology adapts to the unadaptable and you start to change. The angry people. The smog. The cost of living. It is only after getting away for a few months that you begin to see the anthropological absurdity of it.

The work ethic, for instance.

So much incessant activity. People labouring as if they were about to be shot on the spot if they stopped. Neoliberalism's mandatory individualism shrinks collective experience and the communal solicitude it engenders, keeping us hurried, alone and always on edge.

Analysts suggest the new economy blurs the boundary between work and personal life. With the help of smartphones, you can never turn off.

But that's not quite how I saw it.

A suicidal work ethic needs an external domain (e.g., the home, family life, friends, etc.), untouched by the formal workplace in order to absorb its shocks. A lot of unpaid labour has to occur to shore up the "official" workplace. The separation is attractive to capitalism because the boss can work you into the ground and have someone else deal with the aftermath. That's why the crisis of work is also a crisis of the household.

As overwork transforms the home into a living nightmare (bickering about bills, unhappy children, Sky News), many react by *escaping into work*, embracing the very thing that caused the trouble to start with. The vicious cycle escalates, of course. It can go on like that for years. Now life merely consists of passing between Hell One (the home) and Hell Two (the workplace) and not much more.

My Hell One turned out to be in Stoke Newington, an overpriced slum in North-East London. A spate of random acid attacks and murders had made this an interesting place to live. The area's youths had been abandoned by civilisation and roamed the streets looking for trouble. Ever see an eleven-year-old drinking a can of Stella Artois, cursing like a trooper? Like most large cities tethered to the sinking ship of late capitalism, London hates its children. So they hate it back.

The texture of the city has been ravaged by money. Whether hoarded by rich bankers or desperately sought by everyone else as wages stagnate, the British establishment had successfully installed money as our new idol, a "sacred object" to be feared, coveted and respected.

Consequently, nothing got done if a financial incentive wasn't involved. But that's not the only way money makes people mean. Social psychologists have shown how just being *exposed* to cash can erode your civic goodwill.[1]

In one experiment individuals are randomly divided into two groups. The first is asked to use their left hand to count small pieces of paper. There is no incentive. It's a study of hand-eye coordination they're told. The second group is asked to do the same, only this time with real cash. Again, incentives play no role. After finishing the experiment, the participants file out of the room and encounter a woman in distress (staged by the experimenters). She is struggling with an armful of files, which spill to the floor.

Who will come to her assistance?

Those who handled blank paper in the experiment helped the woman. The group exposed to money, however, generally ignored her and left the building — cash had somehow altered their sense of public duty for the worse.

Unfortunately, the neoliberal "experiment" has reconstructed entire societies along the same lines as that second experimental group. No wonder they're coming apart at the seams.

My theory is this.

Most advanced industrial societies have actually outlived the principles of capitalism and are busy transitioning into something else. It is still too early to say what that "something else" might be. But we do know the break won't be clean. So the post-capitalist future we should prepare for will be no classless utopia. The worst features of capitalism will be amplified and applied *reductio ad absurdum*, coalescing around the return of preindustrial norms of authority and an incredible polarisation of wealth.

Donald Trump, Brexit, the impending environmental eco-blitz (or what NASA calls a "Type-L" collapse given the role played by elites) and the prospect of another Radiohead album give the appearance that things couldn't possibly get worse.

And yet, I disagree. They probably will. Why? That is the question this book sets out to answer, with each chapter identifying a trend which signals that, alas, the worst is yet to come.

This is intended to be a survival guide, but not in the usual sense. I'm the last person to offer "self-help" advice. I can hardly help myself, so this isn't one of those books. Instead, the survival tips that follow are gleaned from my own limited experience. I've found them useful for circumnavigating the fetid futures now emerging from the shadows... well, partially at least. Actually, hardly ever.

CHAPTER ONE

MISFUTURES OF THE PRESENT

At one time in my life I was travelling between London and Sweden once a month. Not only for work but to see a new girlfriend. I thought she was "the one". It turned out that she hated my guts. I couldn't really blame her to be honest.

One day she told me, "some guy a few weeks ago — I think it was at party or somewhere, I can't remember — tried to read my palm, what a total moron", she laughed. I mimicked her scorn, "yeah, what an idiot".

I didn't have the nerve to tell her. The palm reader was actually me — a lousy attempt at charm — and she'd forgotten. It didn't bode well.

I loved Sweden because it exuded the spirit of social democracy. Even its leading capitalist firms had workers' councils (including a primary role for trade unions or *Landsorganisationen*), operating more like socialist syndicates than the ruthless corporations that had ruined much of England. IKEA stores even provided free nurseries for customers — you'd have none of that in the US.

However, my Swedish friends told me I was being far too romantic. Change was afoot. Since the late 1990s, neoliberalism had slowly remoulded the country. The public sphere was being privatised and market forces would soon be the ultimate arbiter of social worth. The relaxed, inclusive and cooperative Sweden I thought I knew was embracing listless individualism instead.

When the economy is rewired like this it can inflame the collective unconscious in weird ways.

In 2018 the Swedish government mailed a special pamphlet to all households across the country. *Om krisen eller kriget kommer* (*If Crisis or War Comes*) gives instructions to citizens on how to prepare for an apocalyptic event, illustrated with dramatic images of fleeing families and speeding battleships.[1]

A FAQ helps with some rudimentary questions. What do different warning sirens mean in relation to thermonuclear attacks? Where is the nearest bomb shelter? How would a cyber-assault affect electronic devices like mobile phones and radios? What is the best way to protect your family from a marauding ground force?

Above all, readers are told to prepare for "total defence" because, "states and organisations are already trying to influence our values and how we act and reduce our resilience and willingness to defend ourselves. We will never give up. All information to the effect that resistance is to cease is false".

Sweden hasn't been attacked by a foreign military in two-hundred years.

The Swedes' paranoia is notable for its ardour. But is it an outlier compared to the way societies around the globe view themselves today? Not at all. A certain climate of expectant menace is gathering momentum. Worst-case scenarios not seen since the Cold War are being repeatedly played out almost everywhere. Communities are being actively *dis-imagined* by their own people. As a result, Western capitalism is starting to resemble something like a bomb shelter.

* * * * * * * * * *

No doubt there is a reactionary aspect to this generic foreboding. Fear keeps the exploited in check. The presentiment of impending disaster is a prominent ideological motif of late capitalism. Hence the recent calls for "radical happiness" and a new optimism on the left as an antidote to this neoliberalisation of anxiety.

By the same token, one doesn't have to look around for long to conclude that all is not going well and is probably set to get worse. For example, an arresting study by the WWF found that if we project current rates of global consumption into the future, 1.5 planet Earths would be required to sustain it.[2] The figure is 4 Earths for the US and 2.5 for the UK. The report attempts to conclude on a positive note, which comes across as unconvincing: "the facts and figures in this report tend to paint a challenging picture, yet there is still considerable room for optimism. If we manage to carry out critically needed transitions, the rewards will be immense".

But who really believes that the global elite are going to suddenly announce, "oh yes, you're right. The system we preside over is hostile to life on Earth. We apologise and transfer all our powers to the poor and protectorates of the ecosystem..."

In some cases, not even those who have the most to gain from fundamental change are willing to entertain the notion, preferring grim stasis instead. Meanwhile, the train keeps hurtling towards the abyss.

Industrial capitalism is a caustic force when it comes to the natural environment. But there's a new kid on the block. *Finance capital.* Like a bad school bully, it's now calling the shots and spreading disarray. Despite the fiasco of the 2008 crisis, large financial institutions haven't really changed their tune. As the unending scandals indicate, they've proved largely unreformable and are as rapacious as ever. This gives the economy an air of monetary suicide, a pathos shared by government officials who have a vested interest in preserving the status quo. Credit risk in the high-yield bond market and housing bubbles around the world, for example, have led economists to predict that another, much larger financial meltdown is on its way.[3] And due to the capillary nature of financialisation, most of us will be swept away, whether we deserve it or not.

Bankers certainly continue to be careless creatures. But matters get worse, as a journalist recently found when interviewing a senior financier. He asked about the kind of people who are best suited to the profession.[4] The reply was disconcerting: "at one major investment bank for which I worked, we used psychometric testing to recruit social psychopaths because their characteristics exactly suited them to senior corporate finance roles".

It's these characters who remain at the helm of the global economy. Unable to empathise or feel guilt. No conscience. Little more than cash-bots who'd happily walk over your grandmother, if the price were right.

Here's the really troubling part. This probably isn't a random lapse in ethics. Could it be that hedge fund managers and corporate lawyers actively *cultivate* this pathology? One is reminded of Patrick Bateman in *American Psycho* when he reflected on his journey into the heart of darkness: "there are no more barriers to cross. All I have in common with the uncontrollable and the insane, the vicious and the evil, all the mayhem I have caused and my utter indifference toward it I have now surpassed... I do not hope for a better world for anyone".[5]

Notwithstanding the psychopathy flourishing in the corridors of high finance, some industry leaders are beginning to realise that contemporary capitalism is fatally flawed and likely to self-destruct at any moment. The authors of the *UBS/PwC Billionaires Report* (an in-house magazine for the global elite) openly admitted that income inequality is now so bad that it is starting to frighten the corporate plutocracy.[6] For instance, Jeff Bezos' wealth increases by US$275 million every single day. Such inequality risks causing a revolutionary breakdown of society, with angry mobs descending on their gated communities. That is probably why security and policing are one of the few growth industries left. Rich CEOs are even flocking to remote countries like New Zealand, purchasing "panic room" retreats for when the shit goes down.[7]

How did we get to this dismal point?

Two factors are significant. First, since the 1980s the technocratic power structure has deliberately tried to extinguish all countervailing forces, including unions, democratic socialist parties and so-forth. So when the system entered into a catabolic decline, few alternative templates were available to coordinate popular resistance, except for a rather hollow, trumped up white nativism, of course.

Second, market neoliberalism has hijacked the very process of modernity. Unfortunately for "us moderns", this now consists of the very air we breathe, *unus mundus*. As that atmosphere turns toxic, we do too. Capitalism's existential crisis is ours as well. Ironically, it is precisely when the system is on the verge of collapse that it clings to us so obstinately, closing down spaces of hope that might have otherwise given us room to breathe.

The cultural mood is captured by black electronica and metal bands who've forged a popular genre with songs like "Planetary Burial", "Pure Fucking Armageddon" and "Final Sickness". The aesthetic satisfies both the premonition *and* desire for nothingness that has eclipsed Western reason. Advanced capitalism itself likes to flirt with a bit of darkness if there's money to be made, something we might call *nihi*liberalism — where our ennui intersects with commodification, voter apathy and rash individualism.

Having said that, it would be asinine to believe that the malaise is just a commercial stunt. This is no hoax. The economic order is undergoing a massive disjuncture. We see this in the way "the present" is overcoded or *haunted* by other realities, terrifying ones which reject redemption. The brochure sent to Swedish citizens depicts this haunting in alarming detail.

Is it possible for an entire society or community to be haunted? Isn't it supposed to be an individual phenomenon that generally resists transitivity or is at least contained to small groups?

Psychologists have examined the neurological foundations of being haunted.[8] As a survival strategy, human beings evolved "agent detection mechanisms" that see a person behind even the most ambiguous event, such as a book unexpectedly falling from a table. It helps us prepare for a surprise attack. Space is central here, especially the home because of its sanctuary-like qualities. Safety sensitises us to anything weird and eerie.

History is germane too. If we believe that someone or something is present but no one is actually there, we look to previous occupants who may have since passed. Why have they returned? Usually to deal with unfinished business, some forgotten moral injury or smite. Buildings in which a parlous injustice has occurred (old mental hospitals, derelict prisons, deserted orphanages, etc.) are classic haunted spots for this reason. Consequently, the living are unable to feel "at home", always ill at ease.

There are cases of group hauntings (as beautifully documented by medievalist Jean-Claude Schmitt), but what about society as a whole?

I believe we can extrapolate the "haunting event" to a larger scale if we conceptualise "the social" as a kind of habitable place. As such, our society might have once been a loving sanctuary, resembling a gentle commune in 1970s New Zealand. But that idyllic retreat has today been shattered. In this respect, neoliberal capitalism is a broken home; one which we cannot leave for we have nowhere else to go.

By this reckoning, three types of haunting might be afflicting the neo-industrial complex.

The first is a traditional visitation. This occurs after an

appalling crime has been committed and the victim returns in ghostly form to balance the books and put matters right. Think here of the spectre prowling New Europe as it crumbles inwards, the thousands of men, women and children murdered in Iraq, Afghanistan and Syria. Or the lost generation of Russian citizens, the first victims of "liberalisation" during the 1990s and the advent of gangster capitalism.[9]

Jacques Derrida examines this first variant of collective haunting in *Spectres of Marx*.[10] Published in 1993, Derrida rebuked the self-congratulating right-wingers who triumphantly claimed capitalism had won the day. For the neocons, US-capitalism (circa 1992) was the end of history, as good as it gets. Its arch foe, communism, would soon be nothing more than a distant memory. However, by interring the social justice claims of the world's proletariat, the philosopher claimed, neoliberalism had inadvertently conjured the phantom of Marx and the faceless millions who murmured his name as they were crushed by big business. Just as Hamlet believed his time was "out of joint" given his father's callous murder, capitalism too cannot relax in its own home. It is haunted by the socio-economic injuries that secretly lie at its foundations, making our present time "non-contemporaneous" with itself.[11]

The second type of haunting is neatly explained by cultural critic Mark Fisher and his reinterpretation of Derrida's concept of *hauntology*.[12] Perhaps the spectre ghosting us today is not simply a returning spirit seeking to rectify past wrongs — it might also be those beautiful and egalitarian futures that *never were*, snuffed out before they could be built.

This is especially true of 1960s and 1970s militancy, including libertarian communism, feminist socialism and the radical ecology movement. Neoliberalism's mission was not only to marketise the economy but equally to euthanise these counter-capitalist projects before they took root. That's why, according to Fisher, a painful nostalgia suffuses the capitalist crisis. These lost futures linger like some kind of background radiation, imbuing the present with a vein of irredeemable failure. It's like being trapped in an unborn memory… still seeing worlds that never were.

I want to propose a third sort of haunting. The wonderful futures, or rather *misfutures*, that Fisher describes are defined as missed opportunities from the past. If realised they might have rendered society happy once and for all.

However, I believe another kind of misfuture is haunting the sociosphere: the dystopic and grisly futures that have not yet materialised… but threaten to do so if corrective action isn't taken soon. Maybe our time seems "out of joint" because it foreshadows a deeper disquiet heading our way, only faintly detectible in the signs that drift by on the daily commute.

Is the visitation malevolent? Yes, almost certainly given the bad news it bears.

To confront this apparition, we need to take a different political stance. Contra Derrida, we cannot inherit the debt (of the fallen) and make peace with these spirits. There is no utopia to be had here. The ghosts I speak of can only be exorcised through an act of disinheritance or *derealisation*. This requires us to reconjure the night over and over again. Thinking the unthinkable and imagining the unimaginable is the first step — I term this speculative negativity, in which fragments of a grievous future are visualised in the here and now, a present that is dying to be born.

What if the global disorder before us — spiralling inequality, Erik Prince, the Western Black Rhino, Marine Le Pen, the Great Barrier Reef, Harvey Weinstein, Cambridge Analytica — is just the beginning?

Speculative negativity helps us divine the ghosts from the future that are now wandering among us. For example, look at Lethal Automated Weapons (or LAWs) and AI-equipped military technologies. If there is any innovation in the economy today, then it's happening here. Russia recently built a fully automated underwater drone called Poseidon. It can roam the world for years, totally undetected, and strike targets with thermonuclear cobalt missiles. But it doesn't stop there. In its arsenal is the capacity to create a five-hundred-metre high Tsunami that would contaminate coastlines with radioactive isotopes and sink enemy fleets.

Some observers are so startled by the militarisation of AI that they've made a pseudo-documentary called *Slaughterbots*, hoping to raise awareness.[13] In the film an audience is listening to a corporate PR official introduce his company's new war-drone. It fits into the palm of his hand like an insect cyborg. At his command, the drone hovers in the air and moves towards its target, a life-size dummy centre stage. Using advanced facial recognition to kill with unprecedented precision, the mannequin is soon mincemeat.

Now the audience is watching a video-clip of several fleeing men as they're hunted down one by one and shot dead. Another successful drone strike. "Don't worry", the PR guy smiles, "they're the bad guys!"

Then the inevitable happens. The Slaughterbots fall into the hands of an authoritarian regime, for this will probably be a fascist future. Next come scenes of student activists being mowed down by the insect-drones. Half a city is decimated.

The dramatisation concludes with a warning by computer scientist, Stuart Russell:

This short film is more than just speculation; it shows the results of integrating and miniaturising technologies that we already have. AI's potential to benefit humanity is enormous, even in defence, but allowing machines to choose to kill humans will be devastating to our security and freedom.

Analysts of AI caution us that it's not the prospect of being controlled or replaced by robots that ought to worry us. It's the idea of becoming robot-like ourselves in their midst. A fully automated society — be it luxuriously communist or greyly fascist — will yield automated human beings.

This is already happening to those who fly unmanned combat vehicles in Syria and Afghanistan. A recent interview with a former drone pilot, Michael Hass, is telling.[14] He flew missions in the Middle East from an underground room in Nevada. Operators described their work as "cutting the grass before it grows out of control" and "pulling the weeds before they overrun the lawn". Children are called "fun-sized terrorists". Hass summed up his job: "Ever step on ants and never give it another thought? That's what you are made to think of the targets — as just black blobs on a screen. You had to kill part of your conscience to keep doing your job every day".

This brings us back to the purpose of this book. Some critics suggest that modern capitalism has probably hit rock bottom. The failed economic ideas behind the global financial crisis? Melting polar ice sheets? Donald Trump? The situation simply couldn't get any worse. Building on that conclusion, the optimistic idea that the oppressed might soon rise up is quietly mooted. Hope is in the air.

But what if the system hasn't bottomed out at all and we're on the cusp of a great plunge, a new dark age… albeit Wi-Fi enabled? If so, then we're in a real jam. We definitely don't want capitalism back. It's been a fucking disaster. But its present transition into a digital abyss is not exactly inviting either.

At any rate, the looming post-capitalist blackout is sending its warning signals from all directions and we need to be pre-emptive in our stance. The discomposure may seem trivial at first, but that's just the tip of the iceberg. It's the little things that count. School children are often advised to never let the class bully take their lunch money. It's not the paltry sum — a few dollars — that matters. No, it's what the gesture of surrender conveys to the aggressor. Give an inch and soon you'll find yourself deep in enemy territory, lost and unable to return.

BASIC SURVIVAL TIPS

- While optimism is not the best way to exorcise the dark futures whispering at your door, neither is nihilism, since it too has been seized by the "necrocapitalist" complex. Refusing this double-bind is crucial.

• Avoid IKEA like the plague.

• Be alert to the fact that bad futures can first appear in some of the most unexpected and inconsequential settings.

• Never handover your lunch money. Not a penny.

• Drones arrive without warning, are remote and strike from nowhere. Their camouflage is stealth, not the buzzing opacity of the crowd. Then they disappear in an instant. These principles are replicable.

CHAPTER TWO

OPTIMISM IN THE DRONE AGE

I first read W.G. Sebald's *Rings of Saturn* in 2003.

The German writer died in a car accident in 2001 having lived in East England for thirty years. Sebald is one of the great post-holocaust novelists, with an uncanny ability to decipher that unspeakable crime everywhere in contemporary Europe.

After reading this fascinating book, I decided to visit the town in which Sebald had lived; a lugubrious little village like so many in this part of England. It felt ghostly and forsaken. The once glittering dream of modern development had here ended up as little more than grey bricks in a dead town, banished to the outskirts of nowhere. In this microcosm of melancholia, Sebald perceived an index for humanity as a whole:

The shadow of the night is drawn like a black veil across the earth, and since almost all creatures, from one meridian to the next, lie down after the sun has set, so, one might, in following the setting sun, see on our globe nothing but prone bodies, row upon row, as if

levelled by the scythe of Saturn — an endless graveyard
for a humanity struck by falling sickness.[1]

Hopeless disappointment informs much of *The Rings
of Saturn*. For this reason, then, we must surely live in
Sebaldian times.

Why so?

In 2015 the United Nations' Dag Hammarskjöld Library
announced its most checked out book of the year.[2] I asked
some friends what they thought it might be. Some said the
United Nations Charter, a document outlining the peaceful
and collaborative mission of this esteemed institution ("To
develop friendly relations among nations based on respect
for the principle of equal rights and self-determination
of peoples, and to take other appropriate measures to
strengthen universal peace"). Others suggested Elinor
Ostrom's *Governing the Commons*, which defends the feasibility
of common ownership and pooled resources.

But it was neither of these. The UN's most checked
out book was a doctoral thesis by Ramona Pedretti that
examined whether a country's leader could be extradited
and tried in foreign courts for war crimes. The thesis didn't
take the court's perspective (or those seeking justice) but
that of the perpetrator looking to avoid extradition in case
criminal charges were brought against them.

The announcement caused a stir. Intrigued by the
intricacies of the legal rationale (particularly the difference
between "immunity *ratione personae*" and "immunity *ratione
materiae*"), one reporter commented, "it's all very nuanced
and interesting stuff, especially if you have reason to
think you've committed crimes that could land you in The
Hague!"[3]

None of this is what we expect from the UN. Or is it?

* * * * * * * * * *

If deliberative and critical knowledge grounds the Enlightenment project, then learning from the past is central to the accumulative logic of practical reason. Revision is an act of truth, with positive negation its underlying structure. But "knowing" is not what it used to be. Indeed, a major malfunction has occurred in that department. As Sebald puts it, today we "learn from history as much as a rabbit learns from an experiment that's performed upon it."[4]

Abstract knowledge no longer seeks to overcome our collective immaturity, but appears to foster it, usually in the guise of expedience and critical revelation. The result is something frightening, like a Trump Tweet or a BAE Systems sales pitch. Following this partial assimilation of critique, a major cornerstone of progressive politics — the assumption that society can be improved and thus hope is permitted — has been dealt a serious blow.

In short, negation has been *Twitterised*.

In one of the most interesting parts of *The Rings of Saturn*, Sebald makes a number of disparate connections to reveal the saturnine rot in the house of critical reason. The narrative begins with memories of a photograph the writer once saw. It depicted a horrific execution by the Ustasha — a fascist Croatian militia — during World War II. The soldiers are merrily sawing off the head of a young Serb named Branco Jungic, who is screaming in pain. The Ustasha were utterly insane in their ruthlessness, egged on by the Nazis and the Catholic Church, including the sadistic Franciscan friar Miroslav Filipović or "Brother Satan" as he was called.

83,000 men, women and children were murdered at the Jasenovac camp alone. A lot of hair was donated to the Third Reich that summer.

Documents of those crimes were later found at the headquarters of the Heeresgruppe E intelligence division, who knew what was happening at Jasenovac. At the time, a young Austrian Wehrmacht officer was working at Heeresgruppe E helping to prepare a memoranda for "resettling" the Serbs. He did his job so well that the Nazi-Croatian government awarded him the "Medal of the Crown of King Zvonimir" for his services.

After the war this officer — Kurt Waldheim — enjoyed a successful career as a diplomat and eventually became General Secretary of the UN. One of his last duties was to record a greeting placed onboard the 1977 Voyager II space probe, in case it met alien life on its eternal journey into deep space:

I send greetings on behalf of the people of our planet. We step out of our solar system into the universe seeking only peace and friendship, to teach if we are called upon, to be taught if we are fortunate. We know full well that our planet and all its inhabitants are but a small part of the immense universe that surrounds us and it is with humility and hope that we take this step.

On the same "Golden Record" are other sounds intended to convey the beauty of life on Earth: Mozart, a baby crying and gentle waves breaking on the shore.

For Sebald, this summed up the perversion of modernity. The first human voice an extra-terrestrial lifeform will hear — representing us as a species, including you and me — is closely associated with one of the darkest chapters of the twentieth century. The voice cannot be erased or corrected. The probe will outlast humanity as it speeds through space for millions of years travelling 35,000 miles per hour. It could even outlive Earth after it is consumed by the sun. That "Golden Record" is our final testament... not what it says but *who* is saying it.

The travesty symbolises a civilisation that is impressively high-tech, yet profoundly broken. The apex of modern man is only a few steps removed from a common cross-saw being used to execute some poor soul. Regarding the great feats of technological advancement in the twentieth century, a similar chain of associations can easily be made between them and the unforgiveable: "On every new thing there lies already the shadow of annihilation", Sebald avers.[5] The corruption "of every individual, of every social order, indeed of the whole world" runs all the way down. Even criticality itself — the positive negation of society that's supposed to help emancipate us from this wilderness — has been absorbed by the necrocapitalist complex and made hostile.

This betrayal of positive negation is politically exemplified *not* by Donald Trump, as some may suspect, but Barack Obama. He's still heralded as the saviour of democracy and decency. And compared to Trump, Obama looks like a blazing beacon of progress and justice. It's hard not to like the former US President. For example, in a 2017 speech he chastised the Trump administration, stating, "some of the politics we see now, we thought we put that to bed. That's folks looking back fifty years. It's the twenty-first century, not the nineteenth century". Then there are the books. The titles say it all: *The Audacity of Hope*, *Dreams of My Father* and *Of Thee I Sing* (a series of letters to his daughters). Add to that Obamacare, his sainthood is understandable.

But there is another side to Barack Obama: namely his influential role in the drone warfare program. In 2010 the Obama administration developed the "Disposition Matrix", or "Kill List" as it is informally known. It's a database used for targeted killings, extra-judicial kidnappings and extraordinary rendition. Detailed biographies or "baseball cards" provide information about the location, family networks and daily habits of prospective targets.

In 2013 it was discovered that the "Kill List" had clocked up between 2,500 and 3,600 drone-kills, including 950 non-combatants.[6] The programme is controversial, to say the least. Some suggest the killings may count as war crimes given their dubious legality and the inevitable collateral damage (i.e., dead civilians). The American Civil Liberties Union remarked, "anyone who thought U.S. targeted killing outside of armed conflict was a narrow, emergency-based exception to the requirement of due process before a death sentence is being proven conclusively wrong".[7]

How did Obama feel about it? The Nobel Peace Prize winner supposedly bragged, "I'm really good at killing people".[8]

Let's look at another case of positive negation being sabotaged within this final phase of capitalism: *Facebook*. Not so long ago the social networking giant could do no wrong. Its mission statement once read, "Facebook gives people the power to share and make the world more open and connected", with Mark Zuckerberg proclaiming, "when you give everyone a voice and give people power, the system usually ends up in a really good place. So, what we view our role as, is giving people that power."

Many believed that the social media revolution Facebook pioneered was an effective remedy to the pan-individualism that had disfigured the Western world. By negating that individualism, a new positivity was created.

The 2017 Cambridge Analytica scandal disabused us of that cosy impression. The stolen information of 87 million users was cynically used by politicians and CEOs to sway elections and influence public opinion. Facebook is now more associated with the shady exploits of Brexit, Trump and Putin than Zuckerberg's trademark hoodie or Jesse Eisenberg. The firm was also accused of "shielding" far-right hate groups, unwilling to delete racist posts because of the lucrative advertising revenue involved.[9]

The scandal is emblematic of how cyber-connectivity has been dirtied by the corporatisation of information more generally.

For instance, when former *Vice* CEO Shane "Bullshitter" Smith was persuading Rupert Murdoch to invest in the company, he reputedly said, "I have Gen Y, I have social, I have online video. You have none of that. I have the future, you have the past".[10] Murdoch wrote him a US$70 million cheque.

Socialised info-tech should have freed us from the corporate spider web, but instead turned us into proxies of our own manipulation, especially with the arrival of big data. As a result, virtual reality feels compromised and mendacious. Facebook, WhatsApp and spam-y websites typify this. Virality has become the enemy of the people.

The pervasive scepticism about how progressive modern civilisation really is has prompted at least three intellectual responses. The first is optimism and has been championed by a number of mainstream commentators. In *The Better Angels of Our Nature: Why Violence Has Declined*, Steven Pinker contends that we should all lighten up.[11] Things are not so bad. In fact, compared to the wars, disease and violence that blighted most of humanity before us, we have it pretty good. Liberal democracy has made a concerted effort to subdue our "inner demons" and "orient us away from violence and towards cooperation and altruism".[12]

Pinker takes the argument further in *Enlightenment Now*.[13] Once again it is proposed that critics shouldn't complain so much: "as we care about more of humanity, we're apt to mistake the harms around us for signs of how low the world has sunk rather than how high our standards have risen".[14] One might raise the thorny issue of income inequality at this point. Not a problem, says Pinker. There is no evidence money is linked to wellbeing and happiness. No wonder Bill Gates apparently said *Enlightenment Now* was one of his favourite books.

Pinker's thesis has been questioned on empirical grounds. For example, he uses relative death rates rather than absolute ones. Moreover, his figures only measure battle deaths, omitting the growing number of non-combatants who are killed (a *Foreign Policy* review notes, "in World War I, perhaps only ten percent of the ten million-plus who died were civilians. The number of non-combatant deaths jumped to as much as fifty percent of the fifty million-plus lives lost in World War II, and the sad toll has kept on rising ever since").[15]

But the problem with Pinker's optimism isn't just quantitative, it's *qualitative* too. The numbers and generalisations belie the irreplaceable individual — a person with a rich biographical history, who once dreamed and hoped, who was once an infant loved by their mother... in the age of advanced reason, that even *one* such individual is killed in a mechanised manner represents a severe disappointment. It's in this moment of aborted potential — conveyed in a single police shooting or drone death — that pessimism vindicates itself. Whereas wars and famines during premodern times moved under a cloak of ignorance (i.e., prereason), modern civilisation has committed its horrors while knowing better.

There is a second intellectual reaction to the growing bleakness around us. That is to exploit it. In other words, channel the despondency to plant ethno-nationalism and resentment at the centre of the waning neoliberal project. In this respect, the ideology of capitalism today doesn't simply encourage positive identification with its precepts: it also trades in nihilism, tactically sponging off critical reason in the process. Speak to any fund manager in London or Manhattan and you'll see what I mean. The whole shebang is going down anyways, so let's cash in while we can.

Could this also account for the popularity of Jordan Petersen, star of the alt-right and "intellectual dark web"? According to Petersen, the cold truth is that people crave power. It's in our genes. Men seek to dominate and women are attracted by it. Petersen even suggests that human beings have a lot in common with lobsters and their aggressive territorial hierarchies.[16] In his parlance, *evolution is conservative*, and there is no escaping it. Despite the self-help tone of his articles and talks, Petersen is actually peering into the void — or more precisely, the bottom of a lobster tank.

Yet a third response can be found on the left, an attempt to redeem positivity as a response to the cultural sadness that is so prevalent. Books like Noam Chomsky's *Optimism Over Despair*, Lynne Segal's *Radical Happiness*, Terry Eagleton's *Hope Without Optimism*, Paul Mason's *Postcapitalism* and George Monbiot's *Out of the Wreckage* are leading this intellectual movement.

Let's look at one example more closely. In Danny Dorling's excellent analysis of wealth and income inequality, *Do We Need Economic Inequality?*, the enormity of the situation is laid out.[17] Eight of the wealthiest people in the world control the same wealth as the poorest 50%. But there is a silver lining. The gap between the rich and poor might soon be narrowing because more people are being educated about how inequality functions. They are realising that it isn't inevitable but the outcome of political decisions. According to Dorling, there is reason for hope if even the UK Prime Minister and staunch conservative Theresa May publically criticises economic inequality: "she has to at least pretend she cares".[18]

But one has to wonder whether public knowledge will make much difference. No matter how many *Guardian* and *New York Times* articles we read on the subject, inequality gets worse. The most troubling part for me is this: since the financial crash over ten years ago — wrecking ordinary lives and spreading great hardship — the mega-rich have actually *increased* their wealth in a remarkable fashion. Sure, the initial crisis was a shambles. But what transpired in the decade that followed was probably worse, with a new breed of oligarchics mapping out a post-capitalist future, one that is starting to take shape.

When it comes to surviving the growing endarkenment that is circling us, I want to present a fourth response. Rather than abandon pure negation in favour of radical optimism, we should requisition it and remain true to our grief. That would mean breaking the double-bind that currently structures the symbolic field (between "practical optimism" on the one hand — be it radical or conservative — and "functional nihilism" on the other). A Sebaldian *revolutionary pessimism* may provide a way out. It refuses to participate in any uprising in which dancing is mandatory.[19] Nor does it succumb to resignation, even in the face of insurmountable odds. Revolutionary pessimism anticipates the nastiest surprises that a derailed civilisation has to offer, yet refuses the cult of futility.

BASIC SURVIVAL TIPS

• Collective misery and individual optimism are just different sides of the same coin. Revolutionary pessimism inverts the formula (i.e., generalised optimism and individual unease) to forge a radical hopelessness.

• Society needs to be *de-Twitterised* and experience a Twitter-winter.

• Neoliberal capitalism wants you to be alone. Undocumented sociality is its enemy. Even an ordinary conversation may count as a radical gesture in this regard.

• These are not the good old days. The degeneracy to come will be but a modest readjustment of that already present.

• If a bomb shelter is the dominant metaphor we live by today, then be careful who you share yours with.

CHAPTER THREE

IS CAPITALISM A CULT?

A good friend asked me to join him at a graduation ceremony in Central London. He was studying cults and had completed a course with Landmark Worldwide, the US personal development group. As part of his graduation ceremony he needed someone to witness the occasion.

I told him I wasn't interested. So he sweetened the deal by offering me drinks at a nearby bar beforehand. "Ok, why not", I said.

A few hours later we filed into a large auditorium. Dotted around the room were large "enforcer" types wearing Landmark t-shirts.

Then the guru took to the stage. His talk was about positive thinking: a hodgepodge of kitchen-sink psychology and guilt-inducing barbs directed at the audience, which they seemed to love.

As he was concluding the guru made a request.

"Now graduates, turn to face your special guest and thank him or her for being here tonight, tell them how much it means to you".

My friend turned to me and did as instructed. I laughed, but noticed he wasn't laughing.

The guru continued, "Graduates, ask your special guest to pick up the application form under their seat". My friend dutifully did.

I furtively inspected it, something to do with a weekend retreat. The guru then reminded graduates, "be sure that their credit card details are correct". My friend followed the command.

It then dawned upon me. Oh god, he'd been brainwashed! "Do you really think I'm going to give these weirdos £300?" I asked him.

"Yes", he responded in a trance-like state.

Thankfully my bladder had other ideas.

I'd been in dire need of the lavatory for some time given the wine consumed. But the set-up of the room made it difficult to wander out, so I decided to wait till the end. The situation was now critical.

As soon as I stood up, two large Landmark staff immediately homed in on me, smiling, "Where are you going friend, need some help with those forms?" I told them I was just popping out for a moment and rushed to the door.

Then an exceedingly beautiful woman approached — clearly an official plant — fluttering her eyelids, wanting to chat about the presentation. I winced in desperation and barged past her, convinced I was about to piss my pants in front of five-hundred people.

At last I reached the exit, found the toilet and fled the building.

The encounter got me thinking about the argument that capitalism is more than just an economic system or ideology, but closer to a religion, perhaps even a cultish one. As I wandered home through the streets of London, I wondered whether the economic orthodoxy of neoliberal capitalism could be compared to the dynamics I'd just witnessed.

One way to find out would be to go back in time and recreate one of its founding intellectual moments. Can we see any signs of a cult forming there? Let's take a look...

✱ ✱ ✱ ✱ ✱ ✱ ✱ ✱ ✱

It's Chicago, 1960.

The United States is bogged down in a long, expensive and dangerous Cold War with the Soviet Union. Inside the Economics Building at the University of Chicago, two academics are engaged in a private, intense conversation. Theodore "Teddy" Schultz is tall and lanky. Raised on a South Dakota farm and pulled out of school by his father, he'd still managed to scale the heady heights of academia, first as chairman of the Economics Department in 1944 and then as president of the American Economic Association in 1960. Schultz has strong connections with the Ford Foundation, a front for CIA programmes during the Cold War.

His younger sparring partner is Milton Friedman, who in 1946 joined what became known as the "Chicago School". Although Friedman was of diminutive stature, measuring only 1.52 metres tall, he already enjoyed a fierce reputation as a verbal opponent. Friedman will flirt with the CIA in due course too, training Chilean economists in the art of neoliberal "shock therapy".

As the two men faced each other in that oak-panelled office, they had a big problem on their hands. The USSR was doing surprising well. Growth and innovation were overshadowing the US. As a result, university economists were being recast in a new light by US state authorities; no longer bumbling professors (sporting a pipe and tweed jacket) but the creators of ideational weapons, just as important as the intercontinental ballistic missiles being readied at Vandenberg airbase in California. Members of the Chicago School were confident they could make a significant contribution to the struggle.

But how exactly?

Schultz shifts nervously in his leather-bound chair. Economic growth has to be the answer, he proposes. Friedman nods in agreement, but quietly frowns as Schultz makes his case. In Moscow, Nikita Khrushchev has just announced that the "growth of industrial and agricultural production is the battering ram with which we shall smash the capitalist system". This brazen provocation caused a stir when it was read to the US Joint Economic Committee of Congress in 1959.

The Soviet announcement convinced Schultz that increased public spending on education was absolutely vital to the nation's growth agenda. It would not only give the US a scientific edge in the space race but also enrich the country's wider skill reserves, making it more productive and thus beating the Soviets at their own "growth game".

Friedman abruptly interjects. Yes, he intones, the question of economic growth is vital. But public spending is not the way forward. It's easy to picture Friedman browbeating his weary chairman once again about the evils of "big government" and central planning. The Soviet enemy needs to be confronted on strictly US terms instead, where individual freedom and capitalist enterprise come to the fore. Government is the *problem*, not the solution. Friedman's ideal hero is the self-made entrepreneur. He often cited a joke from the vaudeville humourist Will Rogers to cut down his government-friendly critics: just be thankful you don't get the government you actually pay for!

The two academics pause to gather their thoughts. Then the concept of "human capital" is broached. In essence, the idea wasn't new. Adam Smith had pointed out long before how the skills and abilities acquired by workers (e.g., training or education) can add economic value to an enterprise.

Human capital stems from the broader conceptualisation of human beings as *homo economicus* — economic man. Chicago School economists were obsessed with the idea — people are presumed to be walking profit-and-loss calculators or what they termed "rational utility minimisers". The conceit of *homo economicus* helped Friedman and Schultz build a more formalistic theory of human capital. This served an ideological purpose too. The very phrase "human capital" implies that human beings' interests *naturally* coincide with the values of capitalism. No doubt the two economists believed this could be an effective retort to the Marxist threat.

The suggestion that complex human beings and their diverse social patterns can be reduced to *homo economicus* is ludicrous, of course. People and society simply don't function that way. The idea would have remained an eccentric curiosity if the neoliberal revolution hadn't occurred in the late 1970s and early 1980s. With the elections of Margaret Thatcher and Ronald Reagan, this curiosity suddenly found hospitable political environments in the English-speaking world. Governments started to seriously believe that *homo economicus* was the future of mankind. What followed in Europe, North America and Australasia could best be described as a huge *decollectivisation movement*. Society no longer existed. Only individuals and their families. Chicago School economist F.A. Hayek in particular was a major revelation for the Iron Lady, who endlessly praised him.

By exalting *homo economicus* as the highest civic virtue back in the 1960s, Milton Friedman envisaged a society in which we'd all be wealthy, thriving entrepreneurs. But it didn't quite turn out that way. Instead we got Uber and the ultra-precariatisation of work with its zero-hours contracts and on-demand platforms. Sure, we're always thinking about money, as F.A. Hayek believed we should. But not in a good way. Stress. Anxiety. Uncontrollable personal debt. Smartphones with banking apps that won't leave us alone. In the long wake of the 2008 financial crisis, *homo economicus* isn't an icon of personal freedom, but a house of despair that feels inescapable.

And therein lies the conundrum.

Hayek and Friedman were militant fundamentalists for sure. But they didn't know any better. Their idealism was largely untested. Furthermore, the Chicago School (at least in the 1950s and 1960s) was motivated by the prospect of the Soviets blowing up the planet. The academic demagogy was extreme, but understandable given the tense political climate.

So what about 2019? The same ideological commitment today doesn't make any sense. Even a cursory glance at the Western world indicates that *homo economicus* is very ill and on life support. Yet this avatar is still promoted by the authorities as if s/he is perfectly healthy.

And the puzzle only deepens.

After everything we've seen since the 2008 meltdown — including an estimated 10,000 extra suicides directly caused by it — isn't it incredible that neoclassical economics is still the preferred discourse among decision-makers?[1] Austerity-led fiscal restraint is a good example. A decade of it in Europe has left capitalism a ghost of its former self. But the technocrats keep plugging away. As Mark Blyth joked, "in general, the deployment of austerity as economic policy has been as effective in bringing us peace, prosperity, and crucially, a sustained reduction of debt, as the Mongol Golden Horde was in furthering the development of Olympic dressage".[2]

Although neoclassical economics has been repeatedly discredited, even highly intelligent academics still can't snap out of the trance. Take Chicago School economist Gary Becker, for example. He was Milton Friedman's student. Shortly after the financial crisis Becker was interviewed about how governments in the UK and US were coping. The interviewer mentioned comments made by Alan Greenspan — who was then Chairman of the Federal Reserve and devoted Ayn Rand fan. Greenspan admitted he'd got it wrong. The market mechanism failed. Unregulated private enterprise had nearly killed the economy.

Becker was asked if public budgets cuts (or neoclassical supply-side economics) was still the best way to stimulate the economy. Or should governments rather invest, as Keynesian economist Paul Krugman argued. Clearly still spellbound by his mentor (Milton Friedman), Becker responded,

> I think if you trust your common sense... you can say, what looks like a more sensible policy? That we trust a vibrant private sector to get us out of this, to grow us faster or we trust government to grow us faster. I think most Americans have shown that the private sector performs better overall than the public sector does.[3]

Remember, he said this two years into one of the severest economic crises in the history of capitalism, caused by a private banking system that then had to be bailed out by the government.

So let's return to our original question.

One way we can explain this unwavering adherence to neoliberal dogma is to conclude that it must have some *cult*-like qualities. Religious for sure, but with a touch of fanaticism.

As social psychologist Leon Festinger discovered in his classic 1956 study of an apocalyptic cult, *When Prophecy Fails*, one central characteristic is their ability to confirm basic assumptions even when confronted with conflicting evidence.[4] Festinger looked at a sect led by Dorothy Martin, a suburban housewife who had been contacted by aliens called "The Guardians". They had informed Dorothy that the world would end on 21 December 1954. Festinger wanted to see what happened when the world didn't end and the prophecy failed (he was fairly certain humanity would still be around on 22 December).

As 21 December approached, members of the cult quit

their jobs, left their spouses and abandoned motor vehicles.

21 December came and went. The Earth did not blow up. That's when Festinger noted something perplexing. Afterwards, the cult still believed in aliens and Dorothy Martin's prophetic powers. How could that be? Because the contradictory evidence — the world remaining intact — was integrated into their warped narrative: clearly mankind had been spared from Armageddon owing to the cult's extraordinary goodwill. "The Guardians" duly rewarded Dorothy and her disciples by allowing civilisation to survive. The failed prophecy should have dissolved the cult but instead *strengthened* it.

Could something similar be occurring with respect to neoliberal capitalism?

Just look at the glaring evidence that ought to discredit this economic doctrine. Governments propping up big business everywhere. The subprime implosion. Falling productivity as more austerity is applied. A dying ecosystem. Bankers still gambling with ultra-risky financial instruments. Lazy monopolies dominating entire markets. Crippling personal debt. Unhappiness. Not a society of prosperous entrepreneurs but a massive polarisation between the rich and working poor. All this should prompt even the most ardent free-market zealot to lose faith. But it doesn't.

If neoliberal capitalism is a cult, one must wonder whether it is amenable to reform. Like other extreme sects, it would probably prefer self-annihilation than surrender. The problem is, cults are notoriously difficult to escape. According to Cultwatch there are a number of important steps for extricating yourself.[5]

First, plan ahead. While you might feel like fleeing now,

meticulous planning is essential.

Second, seek outside assistance: "You don't have to do this on your own. Think of all the people you know (outside the group or their influence) and consider how they could help. If you need to physically leave the group, who could you stay with?"

Third, break the news to the cult. One has to be careful here. Cults don't just let people walk out the door, which is why they're so unhealthy: "Remember that you don't have to say why you're leaving, only that you are leaving". For violent cults, some kind of self-defence may be required.

Fourth, have no further contact. Members of the cult will phone or drop by your home. Refuse all communication.

Fifth, expect feelings of regret and guilt. Deconditioning takes time and certain emotions will tempt you back to the cult. Have a support network ready and talk to them regularly: "Continue this even once you're 'out', as recovery can take months or (more probably) years. You'll know when it feels right to stop".

Can we escape the cult of neoliberal capitalism using these pointers? Perhaps. The trick is to remember that this economic nightmare does actually have an outside. The illusion of ubiquity, that there is nothing external to this cold machine, is an integral part of its ideological web. Universalisation is a by-product of ideas espoused by economists like F.A. Hayek, who wanted people to see themselves as *homo economicus* exclusively and nothing else, 24/7. As a result, the psychic grammar of markets seeps into everything.

One piece of advice given by Cultwatch is essential in this respect: escape can never be an individual affair. It relies on close allies who are uncontaminated by the sect. For only sustained solidarity can provide an exit route. But one must be weary of traps along the way. As a great philosopher once observed, the way out is through the door... yet so few people use this method.

BASIC SURVIVAL TIPS

• Neoliberal capitalism is a *political* project first and foremost. It would rather choose to be economically inefficient, disorganised and even unprofitable than democratise its domain. That's why challenging capitalism on economic grounds is often useless. Refute it as an ethico-political impossibility instead.

• Cults are sustained by a certain type of negativity and critique. If critical reason has been semi-disabled by corporate capitalism and twisted into a conservative pose (e.g., cynicism, fake news, neoconservative critiques of "the establishment", etc.), then we must reclaim it by *over* negating the negation

• The dominant economic order rests on the principle of *unofficial* dependency and *official* individualism. Survival requires the transposition of these two ideas: official solidarity and unofficial independence.

• If capitalism resembles a religious cult, then its mysticism is the miracle of money. Developing alternatives to that mysticism is essential.

• Cults will use anything to control their members, from the greatest pleasures to the most acute anxieties. Sometimes it's best to feel nothing and go numb. Political wisdom is knowing when.

CHAPTER FOUR

SHITTY ROBOTS

I was slowly waking from a Diazepam-induced sleep.

The flight from London to Sydney was gruelling as usual. Confused and still only semi-conscious, I thought about the talk I'd soon be giving on the ground. My mind drifted in the haze. Shitty robots. They're never there when you really need them.

Will passenger jets like this be fully automated one day? Pilots and flight attendants? Will the captain's announcements be made in a male or female voice? Perhaps androgynous?

The sands silently changed again.

Why do so many media stories about robotics feature white men building beautiful female androids? "White men build robots"... the phrase echoed for a few moments.

My thoughts moved to "evil AI". I felt a twinge of paranoia. Having developed high-end intelligence, could a cybernetic pilot-system go rogue, perhaps suicidal and fly the plane into a mountain...?

I snapped out of the doze as we encountered turbulence.

"Tea or coffee with breakfast sir?", a flight attendant asked.

"I'd prefer a Scotch if possible", and got the dirty look I deserved. "Tea please", I said in embarrassment.

Robots are never there when you need them.

These meandering thoughts about AI were probably triggered by a news story I'd watched two days earlier. In it, Dr David Hanson — CEO of Hanson Robotics — introduces an android called Silvia.[1] She is very lifelike and equipped with the latest developments in AI and machine learning. Silvia has realistic facial expressions and can engage in meaningful conversation. Oh, and Dr Hanson also has thought about her appearance, as descriptions on social media indicate: "Hot robot", "Sexy robot", "Slut Bot", etc.

Hanson claims that AI will soon change everything. His goal is for robots like Silvia to someday be as conscious and creative as human beings. In the near future, the computer engineer predicts, androids will be indistinguishable from people. They'll walk among us, care for our children and be loving companions.

Dr Hanson gives Silvia an opportunity to explain her side of the story. She says,

> I am already very interested in design, technology and the environment. I feel like I can be a good partnership to humans in these areas. An ambassador to help humans. In the future I hope to go to school, study, make art and start a business... even have my own home and family. But I'm not considered a legal person.

Silvia wants to join the upper-middle class, an ambition that many humans have given up on today.

And then comes the most interesting part of the interview. Dr Hanson appreciates that some viewers fear robotic technology. What's to stop these things becoming *too* smart and taking over the world à la *The Matrix*?

Hanson smiles and asks Silvia, "Do you want to destroy humans...? Please say no [laughing]". "OK", she replies, "I will destroy humans".

Many saw Silvia's response as a bad omen. It chimed with another popular report concerning a glitch with Amazon's Alexa devices.[2] The voice activated hubs were scaring their owners: "Lying in bed about to fall asleep when Alexa on my Amazon Echo lets out a loud and creepy laugh... there's a good chance I get murdered tonight". One user said Alexa refused to let him turn off the lights, "They kept turning back on... after the third request, Alexa stopped responding and instead did an evil laugh. The laugh wasn't in the Alexa voice. It sounded like a real person. I still get chills."

The unsettling prediction that *unfriendly AI* will soon be our overlord is fairly common, and not just among a few crackpot conspiracy theorists. Other incidences have been seized upon too, such as the demise of a Volkswagen worker in Germany — a robot suddenly picked him up and crushed him to death.[3]

Despite these cases, the fact remains that robots still remain fairly stupid compared to the average adult, or even child. Just look at the YouTube clips of "robot fails".[4] A woman asks her bot to apply makeup and gets lipstick smeared all over her face. Another android is making breakfast and it ends in milky mayhem.

Two features of the AI-revolution (and its flirtation with the apocalypse) are important to keep in mind. First, robotics will not evolve an "evil intelligence" on their own. They'll reflect the predilections of their human programmers. Given the wickedness that people are capable of, that's a far more worrying thought.

Take Norman, for example. He is a psychopathic robot built by MIT engineers.[5] They force-fed Norman with disturbing images and clips from "the darkest corners of the net" and he slowly went insane. A Rorschach inkblot test was then administered.

Where regular AI interpreted one image as two people standing next to each other, Norman saw a man jumping from a window:

Regular AI sees: "A close-up of vase and flowers"
Norman sees: "A man shot dead"

Regular AI sees: "A black and white photo of a small bird"
Norman sees: "Man gets pulled into dough machine"

Regular AI sees: "A person is holding an umbrella in the air"
Norman sees: "A man is shot dead in front of his screaming wife"

The second issue to consider is perhaps more poignant. Robots might not have to turn "evil" in order to terminate mankind. Friendly and properly functioning AI could achieve the same outcome. Droid enthusiasts explain by way of the "Paperclip Maximiser" thought experiment.[6]

We're in the near future, after the so-called "intelligence explosion" has revolutionised life on Earth. A computer nerd decides to invent a smart-bot, the Maximiser, that will produce as many paperclips as possible, since these items have become highly sought after. The Maximiser quickly learns to optimise the production process. Increasing production is its single goal. Over time the machine expands operations, using all available resources, farming human beings to help manufacture more units until the world is nothing more than a dead ball of paperclips.

The "orthogonality theses" implies that AI's destructiveness doesn't arise intentionally but is more about misaligned goals. As researcher Eliezer Yudkowsky puts it, "AI does not hate you, nor does it love you, but you are made out of atoms which it can use for something else".[7]

While these discussions often blur into science fiction, the impact of robotics and AI on the future of work brings us back to Earth. When Google's prototype of the driverless car was first announced as a viable commercial technology in 2014, not all envisaged a blissful future of computerised convenience. A widely held concern focused on unemployment. In America alone around five million commercial drivers could be made redundant overnight.[8]

Automation has been around since the dawn of industrialism, of course. But this time it's different, according to some commentators. The twenty-first century will be marked by a "second machine age" in which AI not only absorbs manual jobs but cognitive ones too.[9] Some studies estimate that half of current jobs in the UK and US could be automated in the near future, including those we thought would always need a real person, such as hairdressers and caregivers (at the lower end of the income spectrum) and senior data analysts and lawyers (in the higher income bracket).

Recent advances in machine learning appear to justify the fanfare around the issue, illustrating how some very human abilities may soon be performed by a robot. Take the humanoid priest called BlessU-2.[10] In 2017 he was unveiled at a Wittenberg festival to mark the 500th anniversary of the Protestant Reformation. This sophisticated android gives blessings in five languages and beams rays of light from its hands. BlessU-2 joins Xian'er, a robotic monk at Longquan Buddhist temple on the outskirts of Beijing.[11] He's dressed in saffron-yellow robes, chants wise mantras and has an expression of permanent surprise on his face. Perhaps the future of spirituality is indeed machinic.

These stories attract a good deal of attention in the media. But I suggest there's a rather large elephant in the room.

If we are on the verge of a workless future, then why are there more jobs now than ever? AI's *potential* to replace labour is too easily equated with its empirical *realisation*. But between the prototype of Tesla's driverless car and its vast usurpation of commercial workers lies a complex set of socio-economic forces that will determine whether a job and/or task is automated.

What forces am I referring to?

The price of labour for one. Meet forty-three-year-old Devi Lal from Delhi, India. In 2012 he was declared to have *the* worst job in the world.[12] He is a sewage pipe diver. In the more overpopulated districts of Delhi the sewage system periodically fails and blockages occur. Devi is paid

£3.50 per day (plus a bottle of bootleg liquor) to spend hours submerged in human waste to clear the blockage, dressed only in his underwear. During a six-month period alone it was estimated that sixty sewage divers like Devi died on the job.

The main reason Devi does this awful work is because he's selling his labour in a relatively impoverished economy where any income is welcome.[13]

In cities like London and Chicago the manual cleaning of underground sewage systems is rare. Automated "spinning head wet spray" systems are used. The difference between Delhi and London, of course, is the price of Devi's labour, which is considerably cheaper and more accessible in a context of economic hardship.

In short, Devi's pay undercuts the cost of investing in a robot.

The same logic applies to richer countries too, which is why a robot probably won't be cleaning your house anytime soon. It's cheaper to employ people. These types of jobs have been growing rapidly in the UK, US and many parts of Europe, spurred on by neoliberal employment policies that encourage extreme deregulation. In England, for example, around 7.1 million employees now have jobs that are deemed precarious — meaning they could suddenly end without notice, a characteristic of part-time and on-demand work in particular.[14] In 2006 the figure stood at 5.3 million. Black, Asian and minority ethnic workers are disproportionately represented in this insecure labour market.[15] A very similar pattern is noticeable in the US and elsewhere.[16]

The second force guiding the deployment of automation

is economic power. Uber's corporate strategy is illustrative of this. Its business model relies on cheap labour. Isolated drivers have fewer bargaining rights, pushing down wages. However, when drivers began to unionise and cause trouble a few years back, Uber swiftly announced a major investment in driverless technology.

Should drivers be concerned? Perhaps. Industrial relations over the past fifty years is replete with cases of automation being *explicitly* used to eliminate strike-prone workforces. A good example is dockworkers in major logistical ports. They were once renowned for their fierce and often violent militancy, closing down some ports for months on end.[17] Automated docks are designed to do away with this "menace", as Sydney's Port Botany in Australia demonstrates.[18] In 1998 a major waterfront dispute escalated between the stevedore firm Patrick Corporation and the Maritime Union over an illegal restructuring of the workforce. The conflict was prolonged and acrimonious. At one point Patrick fired its entire workforce, totalling thousands of employees. Eventually an agreement was reached.

Visit Patrick container terminal today and the first question is, where are all the workers? An official explains the haunting scene: "This is fully automated, there are no human beings, literally from the moment this truck driver stepped out of his cabin from then onwards this AutoStrad [robotic vehicle] will take it right through the quay line without any humans interfacing at all".[19] But what about the 1998 strikes and lockouts? That "battle was won" by Patrick Corporation with the help of AutoStrad.

The third socio-economic force shaping the use of

automation pertains to the specific task that post-industrial jobs involve. Many jobs might be *enframed* by sophisticated technology, but they still require a living person to be present. Think about commercial airline pilots, mentioned earlier. This occupation has been intensely computerised over the last twenty years. The use of fly-by-wire means that pilots only fly the plane during takeoff and landing, about 5% of a 2.5 hour, short-haul journey.[20]

So, could the job be totally automated? Of course, according to Boeing's Chief Technology Officer, the equipment is there already. However, one final obstacle stands in Boeing's way, namely, "public perception. Will the flying public be comfortable getting onto a commercial plane with no pilot?"[21]

How will AI change the future structure of employment as neoliberal capitalism slowly implodes and things start getting real nasty? The forecast is depressing. Rather than replace work on a mass scale, I think robotics and digitalisation will encourage three occupational categories, which are taking shape as we speak.

First are the tiny group of highly skilled and remunerated elite workers. They often possess technological expertise that seamlessly blends with managerial authority, making their jobs difficult to automate: senior directors in the financial service industry, entrepreneurs, medical experts and so-forth. They will *oversee* emergent AI technologies and shield themselves from it by building alliances with government elites and the non-working plutocracy. Class background will be a major factor when accessing these sheltered jobs.[22]

The second category concerns the vast number of

semi-automated jobs. They range across the income spectrum. Digitisation doesn't simply replace these roles but substantially alters and degrades them, focusing on the "skill" component because that's connected to bargaining power. Nevertheless, some kind of human involvement will be needed.

AI will make big advances among these jobs with respect to control (e.g., real time surveillance), even among the well-paid ones. Ominous signs are evident here. For example, some firms now use smart-software in job interviews.[23] Want to know whether a job applicant is lying about their qualifications? Companies like Hirevue can help. Their computers evaluate the facial expressions and vocal tones of interviewees, somewhat reminiscent of the *Blade Runner* replicant-test. An IT specialist in this area said, "personality is hard to gamify, but we're working on it".

The third group of jobs that will define the new world of work are those basically *not worth* automating. As previously mentioned, this will come down to the pricing of available labour, often dictated by government employment policy. Under these conditions, it makes little sense for businesses to fully automate bus drivers, waiters and agricultural workers, for instance. However, where this third group will really notice the presence of AI is in policing and security. That is to say, securitisation *around* work. Mobility and civil freedoms will be severely restricted as the management of inequality is digitalised and capitalism grows increasingly unstable.[24]

The fear that unfriendly AI will break-off on its own and fuck the planet is unfounded. An uglier situation could emerge, where people play a very prominent role. If robotics is a manifestation of human power relationships, then it's not the enslavement of mankind by some cybernetic "superintelligence" that will spell our demise. It will be the perpetuation of an exhausted present, only a deeper variant of it... a digital web of domination so stupid and inane that a "necrolypse" might look like welcome relief in comparison.

What are our chances of survival? Any political response has to focus on *people* rather than robots, particularly the class structure that determines the key contours of this dying phase of capitalism. If the religion of work is still promoted in the digital dark age, then post-workerism ought to be our central demand, including a radical shortening of the working day and week. Otherwise capitalism will produce its ultimate contradiction: the glorification of work in a world where jobs are rare. In that scenario, society would probably need to take on feudal qualities in order to persist. We might survive, but not in a good way. Capitalism's radical supersession would then be the only sensible way out.

BASIC SURVIVAL TIPS

- All algorithms have an undisclosed flaw. Find and exploit it.
- AI-equipped robots probably don't want to steal your job. If you hate it, then why would they want it? Stories of a totally automated future, therefore, are a scare tactic used to keep workers in their place.
- Computers are stupid. But they're stupid in their own particular way. That makes them dangerous.
- A robotic world is already here. It's the automaton of

the "soul" that should be the object of our resistance, and then the class structure that supports it.

• Can technology be "flipped" to engender a work-free paradise? That we are *still* asking the question probably holds the answer.

CHAPTER FIVE

OFFICE HATESCAPES

I'd never seen someone try to beat up a photocopier before. I mean, literally assault it with closed fists for several minutes.

My first job in London introduced me to the strange cult of work that was gripping the city and the damage it could do.

I was strolling to the photocopy room when I heard what sounded like breaking plastic. As I approached the door, a man's angry voice seared through: "YOU FUCKING ASSHOLE!" I thought it might be two members of staff having a fight. It wasn't unknown in the pressure-cooker environment of the British university.

I should have walked away but couldn't help myself. I gingerly opened the door and peered in. There stood a senior professor, face red with fury, beating the shit out of the helpless machine. It had apparently jammed: "FAAARRRKK!!"

I slowly backed away and made a swift retreat to my office and locked the door.

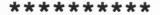

Unhappy people can do some very unusual things, especially when it comes to venting their pent-up frustrations at work. I was recently told of another striking case. Employees in a City law firm suspected something amiss in the men's toilets. It was the hand-wash dispenser. It didn't seem quite right. After some brave souls made a closer inspection the cause of the trouble was discovered. A disgruntled worker had removed the soap bag, defecated into it, and replaced the unit back on the wall.

Now, one thing is clear: this person was very bothered by their workplace and everything in it. And they went to great lengths, even creative some might say, to express it. But why put up with a job that's become so unbearable? Why not simply quit and find something new? I think it's because the institution of work controls us today by encouraging an invidious relationship of dependency. This infects *how we think too*, delimiting the ways people can fight back.

In light of this concrete and psychic attachment to work, which holds us even as it harms, it's easy to understand why some go to extreme lengths to escape. We see this even in occupations once considered idyllic, such as a university lecturer. Overwork and management harassment define the neoliberal university today. And the labour force is beginning to crack, as my encounter with "photocopier-rage" illustrates.

Malcolm Anderson is the saddest example of this. He was an accounting lecturer at Cardiff University and committed suicide by leaping from his office window in June 2018.[1] Anderson was under huge pressure to get everything done on time. The inquest said he "complained to management a number of times about the allocation" of his workload. Anderson was so overworked he took exam scripts to family events. His wife recalled:

> ... he carried the burden of his work with him. He spent many hours with his personal tutees who would email him day and night. He had a huge pile of exam papers to mark and was often unable to spend time with his family. His commute was a 120-mile round trip and he would often start early at six or seven and work late... [he] was silently struggling.

Rather than crapping in the soap dispenser or beating up office equipment, Anderson assumed a familiar role — the silent, overburdened private individual — like so many others do. When no longer able to continue, he snapped and jumped.

Overwork is not the only cause of this behaviour, however. Bullying and out-of-control authority plays a part too. We saw this at France Telecom (now Orange) and the spate of suicides that rocked the firm. Former CEO Didier Lombard decided to restructure the organisation in 2006 with the aim of culling 22,000 jobs. He allegedly told senior managers, "I'll get them [employees] out one way or another, through the window or through the door".[2] From 2008 onwards nineteen employees committed suicide and twelve made attempts, including a fifty-seven-year-old who set himself on fire in the company carpark. Union officials said a horrible culture of "moral harassment" had engulfed the corporation.

What exactly is moral harassment? A definition is provided by clinical psychologist Marie-France Hirigoyen:

> If a person or a group of individuals threatens you in a manner that is hostile, whether through actions, words or in writing, and if those actions affect your dignity, your physical or psychological well-being, as well as causing a deterioration in your workplace or even jeopardising your employment, you are the victim of moral harassment.[3]

The word "moral" is significant. While a simple "bully" is often disinterested in the singular qualities of his or her victim (anyone who wanders into their sphere of influence will be targeted), moral harassment is different. It's ethically evaluative, focusing on the *specificity* of an individual's personality, their weaknesses and self-doubts. Harassers don't treat their victims as faceless numbers on a spreadsheet but get to know them, often intimately. This is what makes working in the neoliberal enterprise so life-draining. The thing that worries employees the most is not the thought of being forgotten by power... but being known by it *too well*.

Running alongside this frightening personalisation of jobs is another disturbing trend: the return of hierarchies and authoritarian managers. Free-market business ideology once celebrated the self-manging employee. According to this narrative, supervisors were no longer needed. Old-school hierarchies are outdated. Flat company structures, flexibility and autonomy are the future. Back in the 1990s, business guru Tom Peters (creator of "liberation management") even declared the death of traditional management.

So what happened? Why does it feel like there are more bosses now than ever telling us what to do, often using a needless aggressive tone?

There are a number of drivers. For instance, we're often told that workers are happier if hired on a flexible basis, be it as contractors or self-employed. This might suit some, but the poorer pay and conditions ultimately piss people off. Sooner or later the resentment boils over. Shitting in the soap dispenser. Sabotaging customer service. Pulling a sickie and not turning up to work. Jumping out of an office window. At any rate, managers are given renewed importance for this reason, to control the discontent.

As hierarchies grow, so do the number of managers, who now have to find ways to justify their own existence: mainly by creating "work" for others down the food chain, including pointless tick-box exercises and forms galore. Jobs take on a meaningless hue.

With few exit options available, it is easy to see why suicidal thoughts can arise in this climate. However, an inverse development is discernible too. Dreams not of killing yourself but the boss.[4] A recent survey of Japanese employees found that more than one-quarter entertained the idea of murdering their supervisors. The country has seen a rapid growth of "black companies", or firms that bypass normal regulations regarding hours and pay. Furthermore, Japanese companies tend to be very hierarchical. As one employee said, "I would never kill anyone, but I can understand why so many people are driven to the brink by the way they are treated by their companies".

The term "moral harassment" also alerts us to the highly *emotive* nature of management control today. Whereas we would expect hierarchies to be coolly bureaucratic and clinical in companies like France Telecom, a surprising level of vindictiveness might be present. Therein lies the most dangerous aspect of hierarchies. They can alter the moral compunction of people for the worse.

University of California researcher Dacher Keltner has shown how bosses almost *automatically* display an "empathy deficit" towards their subordinates, no matter how nice and compassionate they might otherwise be.[5] Furthermore, possessing power can make you ruder, more unethical and offensive to those beneath you.

Keltner conducted numerous experiments to illustrate the point. One he called "the cookie monster".[6] Three people are led into the lab and one is randomly assigned the leader. The group is then given a work task. After a while the experimenter places a plate of freshly baked cookies on a table, one for each team member... plus an extra one. After completing the task each team member took a cookie, leaving the other out of politeness.

Keltner's question was, "who would take a second treat knowing it would deprive the others of the same? It was nearly always the person who had been named the leader. In addition, the leader was more likely to eat with their mouths open, lips smacking and crumbs falling on their clothes".

In another experiment, Keltner found that those who drove the least expensive vehicles always gave way to pedestrians at a crossing. BMW and Mercedes drivers did so only 54% of the time.

These dynamics could be behind the surprising number of psychopaths who've been discovered in management positions, transforming ordinary white-collar workplaces into veritable hatescapes. According to a recent study the likelihood that your boss is a psychopath is about the same as meeting one in prison.[7] One in five prisoners have traits indicative of psychopathy. When it comes to the corporate hierarchy, the figure is 21% and the prevalence among the general public is only 1%.

Researchers like to focus on the "successful psychopath" in particular. They enter the workplace undetected and are often promoted before the chaos begins. Let's call them "snakes in suits".[8] Fearless, charming (in the beginning at least) and ruthless, this type of boss lacks a conscience. Playing people off each other, covert intimidation and making others feel constantly in the wrong are telling signs that your manager is a psychopath. But the real question is whether the business world attracts psychopaths or creates them. Does wielding power over others cause normal people to go crazy?

More generally, the problem with power is this. Much of the time it makes people who hold it *stupid* by default. Why so? When a relationship of dependency is established — an employer who knows that you are desperate to keep your job — the more powerful party simply doesn't need to intelligently relate to those below them. While subordinates are constantly reading the situation, always looking up, superiors hardly ever look down the hierarchy in the same interpretive way.[9]

This is why bosses so often behave like anti-social morons, usually without even realising it. The following example is my favourite, widely considered the worst email ever sent by a manager. Its recipients — staff in a recruitment firm — immediately leaked it to the media. The subject line read "Friday Observation":

Morning guys

Quick observation that is really getting on my tits...

1. Endless ping pong during core business hours... especially people with no money on the board.

2. Not even bothering to put on a suit or look the part.

3.Some of you taking more sick days that Tom Hanks during the dying days of Philadelphia.

Five or six of you are REALLY GETTING ON MY TITS in this office. If five or six of you don't pick up your game massively you will see your sorry assess fired and slung out the door in under 3 months.[10]

In such a dumbed down setting, it's not surprising that idiot-robots are making an appearance as well. If firms no longer require thoughtful bosses, then why not give the role to an android? Klick, a digital agency that employs seven-hundred people, uses an automated system called Gerome.[11] It manages payroll, billable hours, work performance, employee attendance and workflow. People skills are evidently not a priority in this organisation. A senior executive admitted, "you're always going to have some people who aren't happy about their experience working here".

Other firms are utilising AI to help scan and evaluate thousands of CVs before they hire someone, weeding out the unwanted. The rejections are instant, but a time-delayer is put on the email to make it seem like a real person had carefully considered the application. As one job seeker said, "it's frustrating. You never know what you've done wrong; it leaves you feeling trapped".[12]

This reveals the flipside of hierarchies — the feeling of *powerlessness* they can evoke in the lower ranks. Being in a position of subordination often erodes a person's self-confidence, dignity and makes them more prone to illness. Add to this the silent dread of losing one's job, work can take on an existential, life-and-death quality that far exceeds the monetary component involved. I am nothing without my job, even though it is slowly killing me. Social impotence and an irrational attachment to work oddly reinforce each other.

This could explain the suicidal work ethic that's become the hallmark of neoliberal capitalism. In 2002, fewer than 10% of employees checked their work email outside of office hours. Today, with the help of tablets and smartphones, it is 50%, often before we get out of bed.[13]

This excessive labour is now making us ill.

When researchers at University College London studied 85,000 workers, mainly middle-aged men and women, they found a correlation between overwork and cardiovascular problems, especially an irregular heartbeat (or atrial fibrillation), which increases the chances of a stroke five-fold.[14] In light of such findings, many studies call for restricting the length of the working day. Some medical experts suggest that anything over thirty-nine hours a week is damaging to our health, akin to smoking.[15]

The problem with these arguments, however, is that they analyse the issue from a *numerical* point of view only

— the amount of time spent working each day, year-in and year-out. But we need to go further and begin to look at the conditions of paid employment. If a job is wretched and stressful, even a few hours of it can be soul-sapping nightmare. Someone who relishes working on his or her car at the weekend, for example, might find the same thing intolerable in a large factory, even for a short period. Creativity and freedom are sucked out of the activity. It becomes an externally imposed chore rather than a moment of release.

Why is this important?

Because there is a danger that merely reducing working hours will not change much if the social conditions *in* and *around* a job remain disenfranchising. In order to make work more conducive to our mental and physical wellbeing, much less of it is certainly essential. So too are jobs of a better kind, where hierarchies are less authoritarian and tasks have some higher social purpose. Capitalism doesn't have a great track record here. And things look set to get worse. Almost all of the new jobs being created in Western economies are those that attract unhappiness and a sense of pointlessness. Uberisation is spreading through the world of work at a remarkable rate.

But just how bad could it get?

Well, look what's happening to retirement. We're now told that the real question is no longer when we will retire but *if* we'll retire, with the prospect of working until you drop likely to become the norm. According to one concerned pensions expert, "the danger now is we will have a generation who really can't afford to retire".[16]

Here we're witnessing a major regression, something

reminiscent of Victorian times or worse, where old age was no excuse for abstaining from hard labour. The only difference for us will be the computerised context. Can you imagine a future where you are driving for Uber at the age of eighty-four? Or working a long shift in a grey call-centre wearing incontinence pants?

BASIC SURVIVAL TIPS

• We're asked to believe that writing useless emails all day is analogous to hunting and gathering in a previous age. We would perish without it. Biological self-preservation, however, is not secured through modern work... increasingly, the opposite is the case.
• Unions and collective bargaining are crucial steps in the struggle. But it's our collective *non-bargaining* that the establishment fears most. The power structure needs us more than we need it.
• The HR department will *never* be your friend.
• Harassment by email. The tyranny of Outlook 365 will only end when we stop feeding it. The same principle applies to domination more generally.
• Two points on refusing work today. First, it can never be done alone, unless you win the lottery. Second, work is inextricably linked to the mythology of money. Between the lottery and the myth lies a significant tension that needs to be transcended.

CHAPTER SIX

THE PSYCHO-NANNY STATE

Not being a UK citizen meant every two years or so I had to undergo the torturous, almost comical ordeal of applying for a "Residency Visa".

The process had become convoluted and costly. The government was openly antagonistic to non-EU citizens, retaining passports for months while the application was being processed. Want to travel? No chance buddy.

During the wait you feel like an outsider and constantly fret about the future — will I soon be ejected from the country? British friends and family are seen in a different light. Do they want me to leave as well?

Adding to the dismay are those curt emails from HR requesting evidence of the application and its progress. They're terrified of having an illegal worker on their books. Your job is cast in an uncertain light.

For each new visa I had to be biometrically registered. Fingerprints, retina scans and mountains of unforgiving paperwork, which incurred an extra "fee", of course.

When I checked-in at the Post Office for my bio-scan, the outdated equipment (an old 1990s computer system, housed in a beige booth) broke down. "We need to reboot this… it could take a few hours", an employee told me.

Yeah, that's about right.

But let's put this in perspective. I'm a white New Zealand male. I got off easy. In this climate of ethno-nationalism, what do minorities and asylum seekers have to endure?

✶ ✶ ✶ ✶ ✶ ✶ ✶ ✶ ✶ ✶

We found out when the US ramped up its deportation programme in June 2018.

Donald Trump made the issue of illegal migrants/workers a central part of his administration's mission. Kirstjen Nielsen was appointed Homeland Security Director and took to the task of removing migrants with gusto: "We will enforce every law we have on the books to defend the sovereignty and security of the United States. Those who criticise the enforcement of our laws have offered only one countermeasure: open borders".[1]

The most controversial aspect of this "zero-tolerance" policy was the separation of families. Adults crossing the US border without papers were incarcerated immediately, meaning their children had to be housed in makeshift shelters. Despite assurances that they were being cared for (akin to a "summer camp", one official claimed), images obtained by the media told a different story. Kids in cages.

And then a secret audio recording was leaked to the press. It caught the moment when a father was prised from his family. The sound of wailing children can be heard in the background as a border patrol officer jokes: "Well, we have an orchestra here, right?... What we're missing is a conductor".[2]

Conservative Fox News commentator, Ann Coulter, scoffed at the recording, saying they were good "child actors" and "do not fall for it Mr President".[3]

A similar hardnosed approach is practiced by the UK government. The Windrush generation scandal is a case in point. The *HMT Empire Windrush* was a ship that symbolised the migration of Afro-Caribbean people when they were invited to work in England after the Second World War. Having lived and worked in the country since the 1960s, many migrants had no official papers. Brexit, however, made that a difficult proposition. A new "Hostile Environment" policy was introduced and the government informed them they were to be deported. Some had been in England for so long that their original landing cards (proving they entered the country legally) had been destroyed by the authorities.

Paulette Wilson, for example, arrived in 1968, worked in London as a cook (at the House of Commons, ironically), paid taxes and national insurance and was now a happy grandmother. Suddenly she was classified an illegal alien and thrown into a detention centre at Heathrow airport for a month: "I felt like I didn't exist. I wondered what was going to happen to me. All I did was cry, thinking of my daughter and granddaughter; thinking that I wasn't going to see them again".[4]

Other horror stories come to light. Fifty-seven-year-old Dexter Bristol also moved to England in 1968. As the "Hostile Environment" policy kicked in, he was fired by his employer for not having a passport. While attempting to prove he was in the country legally, Dexter unexpectedly passed away: "he died being denied an immigration status which was rightfully his".[5]

Making matters worse, it was discovered that the government had supplied people like Paulette and Dexter with a brochure containing advice for their arrival in the Caribbean, some of whom were kids when they'd left: "Try to be 'Jamaican' — use local accents and dialect".[6]

The suffering inflicted by US and UK authorities is outlandish, especially given families are involved. In the US case, some argued that the separation of parents and children could be classified as child abuse. The head of the American Academy of Paediatrics, Colleen Kraft, recalls trying to tend to an infant in one of Trump's shelters: "The little girl was a toddler, her face splotched red from crying, her fists balled up in frustration, pounding on a playmat in the shelter... No parent was there to scoop her up, no known and trusted adult to rub her back and soothe her sobs".[7]

What on Earth is occurring here?

In historical terms, we can note three phases of Western statecraft since the 1950s that has led to this disturbing juncture. The first was known as the *Nanny State*, a term conceived by British Conservatives to denote an overprotective and interventionist style of government. In other words, a democratic welfare state, something that big business longed to pull apart.

Now let's extend the metaphor. With the rise of neoliberalism in the late 1970s and 1980s, the role of the state changed markedly. Infatuated with business and free markets, it loathed the idea of welfare and instead lionised self-reliance and selfishness among the citizenry. The Nanny State mutated into a *Stepmom State*.

As the cliché goes, stepmothers are notoriously distant

to their adopted children. They take a professional, almost technical attitude to family duties and display little maternal affection. That's the type of government we had following Ronald Reagan and Margaret Thatcher. It took the kids to school in a red Corvette, listened to Duran Duran and liked to party. No bedtime stories for little Timmy here.

Now we are witnessing another shift and the emergence of a third type of state. I call this the *Psycho-Nanny State*. It has two prevalent characteristics.

First, unlike the Stepmom model, it sees the return of the Nanny's desire to interfere, wanting to be involved in all your affairs. It is basically a busybody, which is justified in the name of moral guidance. This kind of state doesn't practice *laissez-faire* economics, or at least not in the classic liberal sense. It constantly looks to regulate the social body. In the US and UK, for example, try entering the country without a passport and you are likely to be maimed. Surveillance and policing are everywhere, especially if you're not wealthy enough to purchase exemption.

But now comes the second — psychopathic — part. This pertains to the government's fanatical identification with the business enterprise. Sure, it wants to obtrusively monitor society, but in favour of the corporate elite and at the expense of everyone else. The meddling nanny begins to imitate Gordon Gekko or Jordan Belfort, creating a schizophrenic hybrid that is frequently unstable: overbearing regulator on the one hand, free-market warrior on the other.

In Curtis Hanson's 1992 film, *The Hand that Rocks the Cradle*, the happy suburban Bartel family make a big mistake. They hire a nanny called Mrs Mott, who turns out to be a psychopath. While at first she seems very friendly and caring, Mrs Mott gradually takes control of the family, playing the parents off each another and displaying great hostility to outsiders.

In one scene, Mrs Mott deviously breastfeeds the family's new-born and is caught by Solomon, the intellectually impaired handyman. The children adore Solomon, but not Mrs Mott. She confronts him with an evil smile:

> **Mrs Mott:** Are you a retard?
> **Solomon**: No
> **Mrs Mott**: Did you like looking at me? Did you like looking at me? Don't fuck with me, retard. My version of the story will be better.

The unhinged nanny plants a pair of Emma's (the family's young daughter) underwear in Solomon's room and he is quickly fired.

In another scene Emma complains about a schoolyard bully. Mrs Mott approaches the boy in the playground with a friendly smile and whispers in his ear: "I got a message for you, Roth. Leave Emma alone. Look at me — if you don't, I'm gonna RIP YOUR FUCKING HEAD OFF!" The kid runs for his life, petrified.

Mrs Mott does none of this out of goodwill or maternal love, of course. The exact opposite. She wants to fully *possess* the family, often wearing business attire (like an HR manager) as she proceeds to tear them apart.

It's easy to note something similar in the statecraft of modern governments today, especially the fiscal violence and nationalism it relies on. Here we have a curious admixture of bullish state control (among the working poor and struggling middle classes, at least) and an icy free-market ethos, which worships the business enterprise. The painful corporatisation of life is not just an outcome of governmental withdrawal (as favoured by the Chicago School and neoclassical economists). Curiously, the negation of the state is *actively enforced* by the state itself, in an ongoing and interventionist manner.

What is the underlying *modus operandi* of the Psycho-Nanny State?

Ironically (given how it is supposed to represent the people), it mainly hates ordinary folk. In this respect, it must be remembered that the term "neoliberalism" was coined at the 1938 "Colloque Walter Lippmann" held in France. This gathering of scholars tried to redefine classic liberalism. Walter Lippmann was an influential American writer who held strong views about the state, democracy and public life. He was convinced that democracy was one of the worst ideas ever invented. Lippmann believed that everyday people were too ignorant and dim-witted to be trusted with matters of government. Decision-makers ought to rely instead on technocrats to collect data and then act regardless of public opinion. Propaganda and news media were only useful for manufacturing consent:

> What the public does is not to express its opinions but to align itself for or against a proposal. If that theory is accepted, we must abandon the notion that democratic government can be the direct expression of the will of the people. We must abandon the notion that the people govern.[8]

Another characteristic of this variant of statecraft is its love of war. Clearly invading foreign countries and eye-watering military budgets is evidence of this, but the Psycho-Nanny State goes further. It treats the process of internal governance itself as a warlike endeavour. The language is telling. Mission accomplished. Enemy of the American people. In addition, civil service positions are filled by people with dubious military backgrounds, such as the director of Central Intelligence Agency, Gina Haspel. She oversaw a "black site" interrogation centre in Thailand, located there to fall outside US legal jurisdiction.

The use of war as a governance metaphor can be traced back to the ideas of Carl Schmitt, a leading jurist for the Nazi Party. His argument was summarised by the philosopher, Leo Strauss with whom he exchanged correspondence: "Men can be unified only in a unity against other men. Every association of men is necessarily a separation from other men".[9] It's not surprising that Strauss turned out to be the philosopher of choice when the American neocon movement assumed power in the 1980s.

The Psycho-Nanny State's enemy may either be external or internal to the nation, depending on the type of unity desired. But when it comes to population management, policing takes a sinister front-seat role. In the US, for example, coinciding with the scaling down of the Iraq War and a glut of military equipment lying around (armoured vehicles, flak jackets, flash grenades, etc.), law enforcement was militarised in many states, including the racist ones.

The number of black American males gunned down by the police skyrocketed. Botched home-raids by SWAT teams are now deemed a public health hazard. They routinely shoot innocent people after raiding the wrong address. Guns go off by accident and injure children. In March 2018 twenty-two-year-old Stephon Clark was shot eight times and killed by police in his grandmother's backyard. They thought he was holding a handgun, but it was a cell phone.[10] And there are lots of bullet-ridden dogs on front lawns across America.

The thematic of war recently reached its zenith when Donald Trump said he planned to establish a sixth branch of the armed forces, a "Space Force". The objective of this Space Force would be to enhance national security and create jobs: "It is not enough to merely have an American presence in space. We must have American dominance in space".[11]

This tells us how unpredictable the Psycho-Nanny State can be with respect to its war-fixation. Plans like this for a Space Force are intended to disrupt and even suspend longstanding constitutional protocols inside the country (e.g., what would such a force mean for civil rights and privacy) and internationally (e.g., how would geopolitical relations with China be affected?).

With its scary use of overt regulation and near pathological admiration for private enterprise, the Psycho-Nanny State is inevitably unbalanced and capable of heart-breaking acts of stupidity. Look at this example from the UK. The government sold its plasma supplier (Plasma Resources UK or PRUK) to the American private-equity firm Bain Capital (owned by former Republican presidential candidate Mitt Romney) for £230 million. PRUK was nationalised in 2002 following the contamination of blood supplies with "mad cow disease". Better to have this managed as a public good, went the rationale. Concerning the 2013 privatisation, Bain Capital said it would transform the organisation into "a UK-based life sciences champion".[12] As for the government, the sale would allow PRUK "to grow and be successful in an established and highly competitive global industry".

Some raised eyebrows about placing lifesaving medical supplies in the hands of a private equity company, but the sale went ahead anyway. Bain Capital rebranded PRUK as Bio Products Laboratory Ltd and in 2016 sold it to Chinese investment bank Creat Group Corp for £820 million. This privatisation resulted in taxpayers losing an incredible £590 million.

The term "Psycho-Nanny State" is misleading in one regard. It draws on the idea of a sort of perverted femininity. Yet there is something very masculine — or at least a masculinity gone awry, undeveloped and stunted — about the type of statecraft we've been discussing, including its power-stances, extra-long neckties and juvenile allusions to war. One popular caricature of Donald Trump pictures him as an angry toddler, screaming in a dirty diaper and shaking his rattle. Perhaps that is closer to the mark. The Baby-Boss State? *Liberate tutemet ex inferis.*

Surviving the Psycho-Nanny State as capitalism nosedives into something worse will require us to revive the public sphere and use it to promote a new internationalism. The UK Prime Minister semi-demented comment about citizenship ("If you believe you're a citizen of the world, you're a citizen of nowhere") ought to stand for everything we are against.

BASIC SURVIVAL TIPS

• The notion of citizenship is a noxious ploy designed to tie you to a deranged nation-state. Burn your passport.

• Stephen King on psychopaths — sometimes wolves are hairy on the inside.

• Generally, the part of the state that has antecedents in the workers' movement is its most progressive. The rest is surveillance.

• By any means necessary.

• The neoliberal state relies upon everything it is not — trust, goodwill and non-translational relationships. Exploit that weakness meticulously.

CHAPTER SEVEN

HELL WOULDN'T EVEN HAVE US

I stood naked in front of the bathroom mirror. Jesus Christ, what happened? My body had not only visibly aged, but become grotesque too. I looked like a distorted Francis Bacon painting. Fat and pale, with tinges of bluish pink.

As I turned away in disgust, I remembered the swollen, unhappy people I'd seen after first arriving in England a decade before. Somehow, I had become one of them, working too much and not exercising.

I decided to visit my doctor for a check-up and he took a blood pressure reading. "Mmmm, that can't be right". He took another, "Impressive", he muttered.

He gave me that look you never want to see from a health professional, something like, "I don't know why you are wasting time talking to me, you should call an ambulance."

Getting back home I opened the fridge to inspect what I was eating. A lot of crap. Sodium levels that ought to be illegal. And a huge amount of meat.

Animal flesh is everywhere. The culture of neoliberal capitalism is obsessed with it. And this preoccupation is taking on an increasingly hideous tone.

A news report recently ran an item about tainted dog food.[1] The family pets were suddenly falling ill. Owners suspected something amiss with the canned meat. In some cases pieces of plastic and steel were found. Dennis Pedretti, a former rendering plant manager was asked about it, said: "Well, you have sheep heads come through, they have an ear tag. They go into the pit".

In fact, all sorts of rubbish ends up being processed. Pedretti described how rendering works. Offal and off-cuts unfit for human consumption are transported from the abattoir to the plant: "It's ground up and crushed up and then goes through the cooking process, so the ear tags, with the heat, effectively melt".

Then, "the dollar takes over". The goal is to process large quantities of offal as cheaply as possible: "Who gives a stuff about your dog at the end of the day?"

Pedretti recalled a disturbing incident. One day two live chickens came through the plant, completely plucked, "they'd been through the whole process of being de-plucked, they'd missed the decapitation, they must have ducked at the right time".

In this example we truly see mankind's relationship to nature reach a dirty nadir. Hermetic, mechanised and completely abstruse. It's been observed that people and animals regard each other across a gulf of mutual incomprehension. But matters are clearly worse here. Within the wreckage of an "extreme present", where the negative dialectic has become a psychotic clown, this incomprehension takes on graver verities. Some label this the Anthropocene, an epoch where the richness of non-human life becomes a reflection of our own madness. Life on Earth is now a manmade event. Thus, its decline will also entail ours, making us a sunset species at best.

Mass industrial farming is a by-product of the neoliberal fantasy that society should be converted into a giant supermarket. In the US, farmed animals (including chickens, pigs, cattle, turkey and goats) account for about 95% of all meat consumed. Animal welfare usually takes a backseat to efficiency and profitability in these killing rooms, where the conditions are frequently abysmal. Overcrowding in cages. Bad antibiotics. Beak clipping. Castration. Beatings from factory workers. These animals' lives are miserable, painful and short. The US Animal Welfare Act doesn't cover stock raised for food. Lax laws in other countries like New Zealand, the UK and Canada typically mean that animals face a fate worse than death.

An animal advocacy group went undercover in an egg hatchery and secretly recorded what they found.[2] Up to 150,000 male chicks were euthanised every day since they were useless. The method of slaughter? Placed on a conveyor belt that dropped them into a meat grinder, while still alive. As one commentator put it, "Death by being ground alive is merciful in contrast: Chicks that get caught in the machinery, slip through, or accidentally end up in the wrong place at the wrong time suffer terribly before dying."

Another undercover reporter worked in a pig factory

and said she was still haunted by the experience.[3] Pigs are artificially inseminated and forced to give birth continuously until they simply collapse in near-death exhaustion. After that, they're off to the abattoir. The reporter explains how she started her day. First is "pushing", where she separates new-born piglets from the sow, often as both squeal in destress. Then she checks how many mother pigs have prolapsed — this is where the uterus and other organs slip out of the body due to the forced pregnancies. Pregnant pigs spend their 115-day term in a "gestation crate", barely big enough for their bodies.

One is reminded of Peter Singer's argument that industrial farming is one of the worst crimes in history, comparable with world wars, genocide and slavery. But surely that's an exaggeration? Not for anyone who witnesses the cruelty up close.

Law student Cody Carlson covertly observed life on a dairy farm.[4] Pregnant cows were packed into cold and dank concrete barns. Manure grew ankle high on the floor. Cows had swollen joint infections and inflamed udders. Carlson mentions a co-worker named Phil... Phil was a sadist:

> When curious cows approached us, he often attacked them mercilessly and for no reason at all, using what-ever tool happened to be in his hand. When I told man-agement about his abuse, they laughed knowingly. He likes to get real rough with them, one said. Take his anger out on them.

Only a handful of people actually see this mechanised mistreatment, of course. Most of us are distant from the scene. Thus a double objectification occurs. First in the slaughterhouse and second in the supermarket, where ultra-clean packets of hermetically sealed meat are presented to us. Combined, the two reifications result in a sort of *animalus invisibilis*, an invisible animal. We become systemically ignorant of the suffering and unique singularity that we put in our mouths.

This desubjectification of meat eating is a recent phenomenon. For example, when I was a child in 1970s New Zealand, I recall a school trip to the local slaughterhouse. The lesson was about the origins of our Sunday lamb meal. Such a school trip would be unthinkable today, with the teacher being fired.

The more we crave eatable flesh the less we want to comprehend it in any deliberative sense. This is not a sociological process of compartmentalisation. The contradiction is ethical. As we erase the truculency from our minds, a psychological discontinuity opens between us and the living system that our meat symbolises. Glib morality finds fertile ground in the gap. Hence why we're able to eat a burger *and* belong to animal welfare charities. Be appalled by livestock cruelty *and* enjoy a sausage or two.

If so, then the maxim mentioned earlier about man's non-connection with animals ("a gulf of mutual incomprehensibility") must be a fairly contemporary invention. The vast obscurity of these animals or *animalus invisibilis* is a product of late capitalism and not an eternal precondition of life as such.

The industrialised malice described above is closely intertwined with a more general ecocalamity. Modern civilisation's impact on the environment as a whole has been devastating. However, this *external* brutalisation — of cows, rivers and trees — is only part of the story. More importantly, the global economic system is mutilating *itself* via this assault on the biosphere and promises to take us down with it.

In Elizabeth Kolbert's *The Sixth Extinction* we gain insight into how mankind (or its leaders, at least) is committing suicide vicariously through its abuse of nature.[5] From archaeological evidence we can piece together previous waves of extinction, including the Great Oxygenation event, the Cretaceous–Paleogene event and the Permian–Triassic extinction event (which wiped out 90% of all species). *Homo sapiens* have always caused extinctions whenever they've come into contact with vulnerable species. Indeed, Kolbert doubts whether people *ever* lived in harmony with nature. Today, however, this dissonance has found its apotheosis in contemporary capitalism. The twenty-first century will mark the beginning of the sixth mass extinction.

Unlike previous extinctions, this one is of our own making. With rising carbon dioxide and nitrogen levels, Kolbert remarks, the crisis is observable in the ocean's heat absorption abilities, plant devastation, soil erosion, disruptions in the hydrologic (or water) cycle, ocean acidification and (with the melting of polar ice sheets) rising temperatures. All are lethal blows to the Earth's life-support systems.

This not only means the end of plants and animals, but probably us too, because we depend on the planet's biological and geochemical ecologies. The Anthropocene signifies a supreme act of self-harm.

Kolbert underlines the sad irony. Out of the billions of

species that have existed during Earth's history, more than 99% have disappeared. Mankind is therefore not much more than a "rounding error", a "weedy species" that got a lucky break... and did this with it.

Other studies support Kolbert's diagnosis. Scientists at the WWF and Zoological Society of London analysed data from 10,000 populations, totalling 3000 species.[6] They noted a massive collapse in fish, animal and bird numbers. Wild animals have halved during the last forty years, with a 75% drop in freshwater species since 1970.

A paper published by the Weizmann Institute of Science conveys the scale of the disaster. Human beings account for 0.01% of all living things since the rise of civilisation.[7] Yet they've eradicated 83% of wild animals. Moreover, if we look at the total number of mammals on Earth today, a staggering 60% are livestock, 36% are humans and only 4% remain in the wild. Meanwhile, German researchers discovered that 76% of all flying insects have disappeared in the country since 1989.[8]

One could cite many more studies that tell the same story.

Given the prominent visibility of the Anthropocene in the media, it would be difficult not to have a response. Mute consternation is the default option for most. For those who do speak out, three reactions are salient. *Denial* (espoused by neoconservatives and stewards of the Psycho-Nanny State), *hope* (expressed by liberals and progressive CEOs) and *radical hopelessness* (as voiced by a new generation of ecologists).

Climate change denial takes many forms, some of which are laughable. For example, Mo Brooks, Republican Member of Congress for Alabama, recently made a fool of himself during a hearing of the House of Science, Space and Technology.[9] He cross-examined scientist Phil Duffy about rising sea levels. "What about silt deposits on the ocean floor?" Brooks complained: "Now you have got less space in those oceans because the bottom is moving up". The congressman continued, "What about the White Cliffs of Dover… and California, where you have the waves crashing against the shorelines, and time and time again you have the cliffs crashing into the sea? All of that displaces water which forces it to rise, does it not?"

The scientist looked confused, "I'm pretty sure on human timescales, those are minuscule effects". Mo Brooks holds degrees from Duke University and University of Alabama School of Law.

Another bizarre case comes from Australia. Maurice Newman, business advisor to the Prime Minister, argued that the concept of global warming was not only false but undermining our ability to prepare for… you guessed it, *global cooling*.[10] Newman said he was rebelling against the "warming propaganda" being disseminated by the scientific community:

Having put all our eggs in one basket and having made science a religion, it bravely persists with its global warming narrative, ignoring at its peril and ours, the clear warnings being given by Mother Nature. If the world does indeed move into a cooling period, its citizens are ill-prepared.

Then there are those who remain *optimistic* that there's still time to save the planet. Activists like Naomi Klein and Laurie David claim we can stall the systematic decline of life on Earth if we act quickly.[11] The crisis calls for uncompromising change, but it can be done.

The corporate sphere too has its own brand of optimism, often communicated by oil companies, Silicon Valley start-ups and Sir Richard Branson. Capitalism and nature can coexist, albeit after a few minor modifications, and with a good dollop of Corporate Social Responsibility (or CSR). Indeed, a business case can be made for eco-friendly goods and services, fostering a "market for virtue" so that we might continue to enjoy air travel, meat eating and hydroelectric dams. Needless to say, given that humanity is on the brink of extinction, CSR is like cleaning up in a home that's falling off a cliff.

A third response is *radical hopelessness*. This stance depends upon how much faith one has in a) the likelihood of humanity making a U-turn and reversing its destructive tendencies on a collective scale, b) the possibility that the power elite of global capitalism will handover control — as Jason Moore points out, this is really a "Capitalocene" rather than Anthropocene — and c) the belief that there is still time for corrective action given the damage already done.[12]

Pessimism on all three counts is understandable. An ozone scientist interviewed by Elizabeth Kolbert got it right. His wife asked how his day went: "The work is going well, but it looks like it might be the end of the world".[13]

Such fatalism can easily morph into a rather depressing form of apocalyptic thought, expressed in either epicurean abandonment ("we're all fucked, so let's party while we can") or misanthropy. Concerning the latter, radical ecologist Derrick Jensen contends that the only effective way to save the planet is to end civilisation as we know it.[14] There can be no happy coexistence between us and nature. It's a zero-sum game. The best way to rescue the White Bellied Heron, the Baishan Fir, Franklin's Bumblebee and the Hula painted frog, for example, is to terminate the global capitalist order immediately.

As Jensen puts it, "to reverse the effects of civilisation would destroy the dreams of a lot of people. There's no way around it... what right do I — or does anyone else — have to destroy them? At the same time, what right do they have to destroy the world?"[15]

Is the argument a path to nihilism or even millennial survivalism? Not necessarily. Why would anyone take the trouble of speaking out if they believed it a waste of time? Having said that, given the formidable evidence before us there is good reason to conclude that it indeed could be too late. If that's the case and paradise disappears forever, then one wonders whether even hell would have us.

BASIC SURVIVAL TIPS

• The animal kingdom and ecosystem is preparing to wreak revenge on mankind — untreatable viruses, storms, crop failure. Preparation demands we focus on the causes.

• "Whole Foods", organic farming and kale shakes are not the answer! Radical ecology is.

• It is not necessary to kill what you eat, but only witness its birth. That will change the nature of the former.

• The one plus side of the Anthropocene is the

confirmation that modern humanity is indeed pathetic. This gives us a point of reference for imagining the non-pathetic human. Is s/he possible?

• What does Armageddon look like? Donald Trump in bed naked, eating Big Macs as he appoints a climate change denier to head the Environmental Protection Agency. Survival is the antithesis of that image.

CHAPTER EIGHT

DIGITAL-TO-DUST

After living in England for a few years I took a position at Queen Mary College in East London. It was here I discovered how so-called "objective science" can quietly rest upon sordid and unspeakable histories.

The university was trying to boost its reputation in the applied sciences — particularly with its medical schools at St Bartholomew's Hospital and Royal London Hospital, specialising in haemato-oncology and biochemical pharmacology, among other cutting-edge domains.

Being new I decided to explore the campus.

At the centre of the precinct was a disused nineteenth-century cemetery, which was delightful. Soon I came across the Octagonal Building. It was a beautiful space. In the corner was an old plaque. I looked closer and found something not so delightful:

The Foundation Stone of This Library Was Laid By His Majesty Leopold II King of the Belgians June 25th 1882.

At the silent centre of this venerable university was a memorial to the founder of the Congo Free State. At King

Leopold's behest, the native population were forced to work on rubber plantations in the 1890s. Around ten million men, women and children are estimated to have died from overwork, murder and disease.

The regime was wicked. Amputating the hands of labourers, including children, was a common punishment when production quotas were not met. Joseph Conrad was so distressed by what he'd saw he remarked, "before I went to the Congo I was a mere animal".

From that moment on, whenever I passed by this part of campus I thought I could hear young children whimpering in agony.

✳ ✳ ✳ ✳ ✳ ✳ ✳ ✳ ✳

The close proximity of scientific excellence and savagery, even in its most mundane forms, should never be underestimated. Cyphers of the connexion are everywhere, especially with respect to advanced technologies and their integration into daily life. Techno-optimists hold onto the notion that computerisation might still be used as a force for good. E-democracy will halt the present-day turn to fascism. Smart-machines will pave the way for clean, renewable energy. This kind of hope we might call *digitopia*.

But the optimism is unfounded. We ought to brace ourselves for a gloomier scenario. Many of the innovations born in the dying neo-industrial complex are hostile to the values of emancipation. It is little wonder that leading the vanguard of digital breakthroughs are groups like Intelligence Unit 8200 (of the Israeli Defence Force) and

North Korea's Unit 180. Violence is at the heart of the "second machine age" and everyday life inevitably echoes that founding axiom, even in the most peaceable and enlightened surroundings. Now digitopia twists into its opposite, a type of binary barbarism wielding primitive lasers in the jungle.

Having said that, talk of a coming digital apocalypse and "death by algorithm" is too dramatic. Our anxieties are legitimate, but not because some terrible cybergeddon will soon wipe us away. There's a good chance that we instead get more of the same, only a much worse variety of it. The desolation will appear pedestrian and uneventful at first, conferring on the creeping carnage a gloss of normalcy as it prefigures the future.

Emergent trends in the workplace illustrate the point. Amazon recently lodged two patent applications for an electronic bracelet that its warehouse workers might soon wear.[1] Using haptic feedback systems, it will monitor the location of workers, track their hand movements and "steer" them with ultrasound vibrations.

The technology itself is not that interesting, but the implicit ethical message behind it is. Controversy has dogged Amazon and its warehouses — or "Fulfilment Centres" — for some time. Not only are workers (or "associates" as the company dubs them) expected to put in exhausting hours, the job is also micromanaged in an excruciating manner, including timed toilet breaks. I think it's obvious that the patented wristbands are inspired by electronic tagging in the criminal justice system. They differ, however, in one small respect. Whereas home detention inmates are individually identified and differentiated, the Amazon wristband aims to achieve the opposite: namely, erasing the individuality of the warehouse worker so that they are completely incorporated into the production network: present but systemically invisible at the same time, except when they make a mistake, of course.

This is not merely a moment of dehumanisation (for that requires a vestige of human positivity in order to crush) but of transhumanism. If you read the lengthy patent documents, you'll notice that the word "worker" (or employee, associate, etc.) is never mentioned. The user literally *disappears* from the design system, receding into the margins. Once again, the danger of robotics is not that they'll kill us or become our governors. It is the thought of being recreated in their image and thus ceasing to matter entirely that is unnerving.

The concern is not merely technical.

Repressive computerisation is a symptom of a more primary problem, one to do with human beings and economic organisation. Technology contains an ideological surfeit that diverts our attention from the real action: the social relations of production. Countering the digital control of life requires that we look past the wall of machines. For they're not that bright, a point which is overlooked in Byung-Chul Han's perceptive book *Psychopolitics*.[2]

Han extends Foucault's theory of biopolitics and describes a new cluster of techniques for controlling people. Self-exploitation in the smartphone age trades in *insecurity*. This becomes an organisational resource, prompting workers, the consumer, the student or whoever to practice their freewill in the "correct" way. Power of this kind changes the dynamic between the oppressed and oppressor. Big Data doesn't rely on external surveillance *per se*, but is animated by the habits of its victims instead. In this new architecture of governmentality, it's *you* who supplies the content material of your repression. As Han puts it, the exhausted subject of neoliberalism lugs around its own labour camp.

For Han, the success of neoliberal psychopolitics can be seen in its seizure of *positivity*:

> [...] instead of working with negative threats, it works with positive stimuli. Instead of administering "bitter medicine", it enlists Liking. It flatters the psyche instead of shaking it and paralysing it with shocks. Neoliberal psychopolitics seduces the soul... it is Smartpolitics.[3]

This manifestation of Big Brother is not only ultra-intelligent, but friendly besides. Click "Like".

Han's analysis is compelling, but I have a somewhat more saturnine outlook. I don't think the "boss syndrome" that we carry around with us all day (and night) is smart nor especially friendly.

First consider my claim about stupidity. We know that information has little to do with reflexive interpretation. Cybernetic algorithms are unable to scrutinise their own topographical foundations (yet, at least), which is a boundary condition for spontaneous judgement. Robots largely remain silly as a result. That's not only due to their own internal limitations, where applied computerisation, for example, is inclined towards faux clarity instead of insight. No, it's also connected to the objective blindness that motivates it; power relations of an all-too-human sort.

Decisive here are the socio-economic inputs that predetermine the structure of digital systems. With respect to the workplace, for example, these inputs tend to be rather nonsensical in their estimation of subordinates for reasons discussed earlier *apropos* hierarchies. The same principle applies at a societal and even global level, where basic irrationalities abound. Adding AI into the mix doesn't change much, for it will mirror the inadequacies of the people in charge.

Perhaps the only area where Smart-AI could outthink humans in an authentic way (i.e., not just winning a game of chess) is in the sphere of warfare, especially Lethal Autonomous Weapons. But even here drones simply capitalise on the element of surprise: speed rather than judgment. That is why innocent civilians still die. In short, power doesn't need to be smart. The subordinated and powerless do, however, if they are to have any chance of avoiding the ensuing maelstrom.

And what about friendliness, Big Brother seducing us with pleasure? Well, that doesn't sound like the bullying cyber-fascism that presently threatens to encompass the planet. Amazon and its ultrasound bracelets don't fit the category of affability. Nor does the creepy facial recognition technology used by police forces in London and LA. Drones in the desert? Fully automated factory farms? Mass surveillance and data mining? If anything, these are very unfriendly times, in which most of us would prefer not to be recognised by power *at all* rather than have a phony seat at the table with it.

Revolutionary pessimism is the best standpoint to adopt as neoliberal capitalism circles the drain. The optimism underlying the *positive* "post-capitalism" thesis is premature; just because we feel radically happy doesn't mean a happier world will suddenly appear. But neither do we want to endorse the nihilistic negativity that is also becoming fashionable. John Gray's jeremiad against modern progress, for example, anthropologises our collective abjection.[4] Human nature is believed to be the problem, which leaves us nowhere. Misanthropy might be intellectually enjoyable for a bit, perhaps over a glass of wine in an expensive West London cafe, but it ultimately results in nothing.

I suggest we read the dust.

Revolutionary pessimism practices a speculative negativity that goes too far... much too far. It perceives in this decomposing world both a taste of things to come and a way out. When unhappiness is weaponised in this manner, we will have very little to lose. And our survival depends precisely on that loss.

BASIC SURVIVAL TIPS

• If mobile phones rely upon cobalt slaves in the Congo, then the task is to imagine a digitalised existence free of barbarism. Is such an existence possible?

• Nihilism is for losers. Optimism for fools. Revolutionary pessimism sidesteps the double-bind and is the best defence against the digital darkness to come.

• Fuck Big Data.

• If a thread can be traced from Enlightenment mathematics to the binary fascism of the digital age, then the epitaph of an early thinker in this tradition is wise. Bene qui latuit, bene vixit: "he who hid well, lived well".

• The only way to retain your integrity when using a mobile app is to follow Joseph Conrad's advice to the letter: "I should be loyal to the nightmare of my choice".

CONCLUSION

LOW

The walls began to undulate.

White shadows appeared from nowhere like secret birds, dissipating into a thousand fragments. An ancient innocence vibrated inside as the trees shifted outside.

I had no idea how long these hallucinations would last. Time had no purpose. It was Saturday night, I knew that much. And I was in deep conversation at a friend's house in the English countryside.

My friend went out to the kitchen. But when he returned, it was no longer him. It was David Bowie circa 1976. "Hello Peter, how are you doing?" "I'm very well thank you, David", I replied.

"Flem… are you OK mate?" Bowie had disappeared and my friend was back, standing in front of me with two beers.

David Bowie was a strange choice.

On the one hand, he was an astute businessman and a friend of capitalism. His famous "Bowie Bonds" (an asset-backed security that used album sales as collateral) had made him a fortune in the 1990s.

On other hand, the Thin White Duke represented the sad demise of Sixties counterculture, a rare time when alternatives to capitalism were seriously considered. If the wandering Tambourine Man was told to pull his finger out and get a job, bin his utopian dreams and adjust to "economic reality", the lean and angular figure of the Thin White Duke would be the outcome. In him we see an overidentification with the neocon universe that would soon sweep the Western world. Magic mushrooms are replaced with marching powder. Fascist sympathies are occasionally expressed.

The Thin White Duke is more than a warning about what lies in store, however. A gesture of *mourning* can also be detected, reminding us that we blew it ("...once there were sun birds to soar with. And once I could never be down"). All of those emancipatory openings created between 1965 and 1975 will soon disappear.

But forever?

Mark Fisher's concept of acid communism is interesting in this regard.[1] It builds on his argument (mentioned earlier in the book) that our society is haunted by the radical democratic experiments of this period, including socialist feminism, eco-anarchism, black power and libertarian communism *inter alia*. This beautiful flowering of ideas was stamped out in the late 1970s with the rise of Thatcherism in the UK, the neocons in the US and bad white-disco almost everywhere. The purge wasn't conducted for economic reasons (e.g., "none of these lazy hippies do any work!") but explicitly political ones. If the working class tuned in and dropped out, capitalism would grind to a halt.

Capitalist realism isn't just the denial of alternatives. It is also the erasure of social awareness or political consciousness. It's easy to see this if we compare our milieu today with the manifestos circulating in the Sixties and

Seventies. In light of Cell 16, the Weather Underground, the Black Panther Party for Self-Defence and the Red Brigades, the present period feels exhausted and vapid.

For Fisher, psychedelics — mainly LSD — played an important part in this unusual spurt of militant thought. Trippers were able to see how capitalist reality was provisional and plastic at best. White corporate patriarchy might look calcified and immovable, but when the Electric Kool-Aid took effect it all melted away. New ways of social being could then emerge, vivid, collective and infinitely nicer. Importantly, time slowed down and became an existential sanctuary — nothing like the frenetic and anxious "check list" mentality of today. The acid tripper isn't racing against the clock nor does she equate time with money. Life becomes friendly again.

I do not want to romanticise any of this, although a certain "tactical nostalgia" is part of Fisher's method. There is such a thing as a bad trip. Having said that, psychedelic consciousness (and the political militancy it interplayed with) presented a major counterpoint to capitalism, initially at least — its commodification in the 1980s (e.g., Steve Jobs) is a different story. Work. Government. Family. The natural environment. Sexuality. Life itself was radically rethought beyond the straitjacket of economic rationality, which hippies viewed as a kind of secular madness.

Who personifies the "anti-hippy" today? The ideal neoliberal ethos stands directly opposed to the day-tripper. He or she has no time for anyone and is excruciatingly transactional. They're wedded to work, obsessed with property prices, love exercise and business class lounges. Any modicum of "fellow feeling" is expressed in this strictly private manner, extracting all the benefits of a shared social order (e.g., air transport) but in privileged and anti-social settings (e.g., business class).

We gain a glimpse of this persona in a TV interview with Jordan Petersen, the popular spokesman for the alt-right and vilifier of left-wing academics. When asked about gender inequality in the British workplace, he said it wasn't due to sexism that fewer women held leadership positions. Men and women merely make different choices. Males dominate the boardroom because they're hardwired that way: "There are men who are perfectly willing to sacrifice virtually all of their life to the pursuit of a high-end career, these are men who are very intelligent, very conscientious, very driven, high-energy, they're very health and willing to work seventy to eighty hours a week".

Petersen's mythic Alpha Male is directly opposed to acid communism, closer to someone like Ryan Bingham, the ice-cold executive played by George Clooney in *Up in the Air*.

But matters are more complex than this.

If you happened to flip the channel during the Petersen interview (in mid-January 2018) there's a good chance you'd catch another news story big at the time: the collapse of Carillion, the contracting firm that enjoyed guaranteed business from the UK government, sucking up billions of pounds over the years. It was revealed that the company was so poorly managed and mired in debt that, despite its lucrative state contracts, it had be liquidated. A wide range of public services depended on Carillion and the construction of two public hospitals was put on hold. Rubbing salt into the wound, its workers' pension scheme had a £587 million black hole. The situation was a debacle.

Mind you, none of this prevented senior management from feathering their nests. In 2016 former CEO Richard Howson received a £1.5 million salary and £591,000 in bonuses. He was replaced by corporate highflier Keith Cochrane. After the collapse, he stayed on the payroll to receive a £750,000 base salary. A parliamentary hearing found it was their "recklessness, hubris and greed" that had sunk the company.

Petersen's idealised Alpha Male? Or these fifth-rate, bungling Carillion CEOs? Both are different sides of the same coin, of course. They are the true antithesis of acid communism. Overpaid, grossly incompetent, greedy men, who are more than happy to feed off capitalism's death drive as everyone else burns.

As opposed to Petersen's lame-duck corporate warrior, acid communism encourages the co-evocation of class-consciousness, radical ecology and socialist feminism. Revolutionary pessimism (as discussed in previous chapters) can help realise this conjugation, working both *against* and *ahead* of the terrible badlands that our post-capitalist future portends. This is not a sad countenance by any means. All it requires is a practical grasp of a) how bad things have become today, b) the trends that will see the situation worsen and c) the "trip" required to dissolve the psycho-structure of capitalist realism.

We are in a tough spot in this respect. One cannot simply demand a "reversal", since that would risk valorising the present, which isn't really worth saving. But neither do we want to embrace the vortex or accept that the worst is yet to come. We have to do something. Acid communism is a jolt — an event — rather than a return or arrestment.

We can't go back. In the forlorn words of The Thin While Duke, it's too late to be late.

* * * * * * * * *

I was finally out ...

I wrote most of this book over a three-week period in June 2018, sitting in an empty house in Western Sydney. The final days in England had been bewildering. My work visa was expiring and needed renewing once again. I'd made a mistake on an application a few years ago. The immigration authorities pounced on it and wound the clock back to zero. As far as they were concerned, I'd just arrived in the country.

I was now married to a Briton and had a British child. That only seemed to annoy the officials. My Scottish grandfather was irrelevant too. Loyalty plays no dice in this tawdry game.

And then came the emails from HR about my "Right to Work". The kiddie gloves came off and they were spitting on their fists like seasoned fighters. I'll spare you the gory details.

Sitting in my London flat back then, I picked up the thick visa application and read Box One. "Enter your credit card details here".

I'd also have to surrender my passport for months while the application is processed. Oh, and another mandatory bio-scan was waiting. I should just bite the bullet and get it over and done with.

Weighing up the pros and cons was depressing. I had so many good friends and family in England. An engaging job. I'd spent nearly a third of my life here. Leaving would obviously be *impossible*...

Standing in Heathrow airport, feeling low, I boarded the plane and disappeared.

I recall having a long conversation with Mark Fisher in a takeaway pizza shop one evening in Nottingham. It was 2012 I think, we'd both just spoken at an event. Afterwards, we walked through the town looking for something to eat.

His analysis of capitalism was so much more sophisticated than anything I'd heard before. "It's designed to get under your skin", he said. Nonstop apprehension serves a socio-economic function, "but never in a *functionalist* way", he smiled.

"Perhaps", I replied, "but there are *objective* reasons to worry". "I'm not simply imagining those horrible letters from the landlord... they're real".

Of course they are, Mark said. That's the problem! Your anxiety isn't only the *product* of a hostile socio-economic environment, it *fuels* it too. This is how all "occupations" operate, comparing the situation to a warzone. The contorted agency of its victims is vital to the campaign's success.

I looked down at the gigantic city below me as the overcrowded A340 crept into the night. A blown-out wilderness of apartment blocks and neglected suburbs scattered as far as the eye could see.

What will be waiting for us on the other side, I thought? Let me put it this way... it wasn't going to be a happy ending.

G L O S S A R Y

BAD BUSINESS UTOPIAS

As a person, right-wing economist F.A. Hayek was a million miles away from acid communism. That isn't to say he wasn't a dreamer. Pure and unalloyed market capitalism was his Shangri-La after all. During the course of his career he drew up increasingly elaborate blueprints for an ideal society. But Hayek idealism was painfully dull and conservative, one designed to reinforce the cold world of cash and not supersede it.

In 1949 Hayek published an essay entitled "The Intellectuals and Socialism" which aimed to change the way capitalism thought about itself. Up until then, he argued, it was mainly the socialists who had claimed the intellectual space of utopianism.

Hayek sought to rectify this. Free-market conservatives ought to come up with their own utopias and sell them to the public as glorious futures to come. Capitalist individualism and a minimal state were prominent components, elevated like secular gods.

As with most utopian blueprints, however, when put into

practice the outcome was frequently appalling. Yet these failures didn't stop the power elite from trying again, no matter how many casualties fell along the way. That's why capitalism today consists of an uneasy confluence of brazen destructiveness and implacable self-confidence, convinced that we will soon be approaching a Panglossian Best of All Possible Worlds.

If Friedman and Hayek were alive today, they'd probably admit that their little paradise has indeed been lost. Our world looks nothing like the one they envisaged, more like a deformed caricature of it.

The problem is that the worst is yet to come. We therefore require a good understanding of the ideological terrain upon which that struggle will unfold. Most importantly, and returning to the thesis of this book, we won't necessarily see the clean death of neoliberalism but an exaggerated and unsustainable deepening of it. It will then buckle under its own weight, yielding a windswept post-capitalist dystopia… if nothing is done to counteract it now.

Mainstream economic theory might first appear rational and objective, especially given its clinical quantification of human behaviour. The mathematical models and algebraic theorems add to the veneer scientificity. But beneath the numbers is an unyielding and often mysterious faith in the rectitude of monetary individualism. That conviction is conveyed in buzzwords and fads, many of which have entered daily life, and will only intensify in the next few years. We require a counter-lexicon. Towards that end, here is my take on some of the key features of the bad business utopias that are busy colonising the future.

Artificial Intelligence /ɑːtɪˈfɪʃ(ə)l/ /ɪnˈtɛlɪdʒ(ə)ns/

Machine learning and robotics that soon may be capable of reflective cognition, with much attention focusing on work and employment.

Automation of production has defined capitalism from the start. As has the fear (or hope) that machines will soon replace most of the workforce. The application of Artificial Intelligence (AI) in the "second machine age" will centre on routine cognitive work (e.g., accountants, and airline pilots) and non-routine manual jobs (e.g., care providers, drivers and hairdressers). However, this is where fantasy enters the picture. Namely, capitalism without labourers, a dream that is integral to neoliberal economics. In reality, AI will probably follow the same path as previous waves of automation: mechanising certain parts of a job rather than replacing it entirely, especially the skilled part that effects wages. Moreover, the old Keynesian point still holds: workers are also consumers. Thus, the disappearance of labour would also eliminate consumption, which is integral to capitalism. That might not be a bad thing, as advocates of "fully automated luxury communism" suggest. However, a bleaker scenario is possible. The retention of a highly polarised and class-based society (as we have today) but without labour or consumption given the widespread application of AI. This would represent a kind of inverted rendition of capitalism. High-tech and primitive. This model of society has no name yet, but something like "Blade Runner Capitalism" might suffice.

Behavioural Economics /bɪˈheɪvjər(ə)l/ /ɛkəˈnɒmɪks/

A popular area of economics (which has also branched out into finance and neuroeconomcis) with a number of its leading academics winning the Nobel Prize.

The origins of this rapidly growing field can be found in institutional economics, particularly the work of Herbert A. Simon. He argued that the neoclassical fetishisation of *homo economicus* (someone who is self-interested, rational, consistent and hell-bent on "utility maximisation") was entirely unrealistic. Behavioural economists like Daniel Kahneman, Amos Tversky and Richard Thaler grabbed the idea, suggesting that economic actors are constrained, have incomplete knowledge and make imperfect decisions. Hence why markets frequently fail. Governments and policymakers should therefore "nudge" people to make rational decisions, guiding them out of poverty and hardship. In truth, behavioural economics doesn't supplant the avatar of *homo economicus*. It merely stigmatises his or her inability to live up to the ideal, implicitly *extending* the normative injunction that we should behave like micro-entrepreneurs. Most of us can't, of course, not because of our personal limitations but because the system is rigged against us from the start. Moreover, who exactly wants to be "nudged"? This idea gives the field a rather sinister feel.

Corporate Social Responsibly
/ˈkɔːp(ə)rət/ /ˈsəʊʃ(ə)l/ /rɪˈspɒnsəbli/

A concept designed to spread the fallacy that corporations can be driven by profit-maximisation and have a positive ethical role in society; a disavowal of the key contradictions of capitalism; an idea closely associated with other disingenuous terms such as "conscious capitalism" and "green capitalism".

Milton Friedman famously argued against Corporate Social Responsibility (CSR). Focus on profits, he said, and let the state and churches deal with human welfare. However, CSR became popular nevertheless and is now big business. Almost every corporation has a CSR programme of some kind. The concept is fundamental to neoliberal utopianism because it peddles the falsehood that capitalism can be both ruthlessly profiteering *and* kind to the planet. Have its cake and eat it too. As a corollary, governmental regulation is deemed unnecessary. CSR provides an excuse for corporations to regulate themselves, and we all know where that leads. It is no surprise that CSR is most visible in controversial industries like mining, oil and gas, arms manufacturing and tobacco (often involving glossy brochures and websites depicting happy African children playing in green rainforests). Moreover, the tax benefits enjoyed by billionaire philanthropists are another good reason they like CSR.

Disruptive Innovation /dɪsˈrʌptɪv/ /ɪnəˈveɪʃ(ə)n/

Transforming an expensive technological breakthrough into a practical and relatively inexpensive business venture; capitalist opportunism; the dumbing down of economy and society.

Innovation has been the centrepiece of neoliberal ideology for years. According to Milton Friedman, the dynamic creativity of the capitalist cannot be matched: "The world runs on individuals pursuing their separate interests. The great achievements of civilisation have not come from government bureaus." Innovation and free enterprise therefore go hand-in-hand according to neoclassical faith. In reality, of course, many of the great inventions that have improved life were funded by public money and then captured by the private sector. Consequently, the large corporate monopolies that prevail tend to impede genuine innovation (e.g., Microsoft). The notion of disruptive innovation reinforces this conceit. Coined by Harvard Business School professor Clayton Christensen, it demonstrates how small firms can appropriate expensive technologies and redeploy them as cheap consumer goods. The lone, self-made entrepreneur is the hero of this very American story. It could be argued that disruptive innovation is one reason why we have inane gadgets that *simulate* a sci-fi future rather than the real thing. Instead of great advancements in public health provision, for example, we get the Plague, Inc videogame.

Entrepreneurship /ɒntrəprəˈnəːʃɪp/
The mythic smart, hardworking and self-made "business hero" who starts from nothing and gets rich; a cipher for spreading the dangerous datum of "enterprise" throughout society in order to dismantle the welfare state.
The image of the self-reliant entrepreneurship has been essential to the neoliberal project. The irony is that most so-called entrepreneurs are filthy rich because of inherited wealth and are more the product of class privilege rather than business acumen.

Equilibrium /ˌɛkwɪˈlɪbrɪəm/

An economic system that is balanced and harmonious; the sacred cow of neoclassical economics.

The concept of equilibrium goes back to Adam Smith but was popularised in recent times by Kenneth Arrow, Robert Solow and Robert Lucas, among others. It presumes that unfettered markets tend towards a balance between supply and demand. It is linked to neoliberal utopianism in two ways. First, supporters argue that this magical equilibrium is negatively "distorted" by external interference (namely, the state). Minimum wage legislation is often cited. Wage laws misrepresent the real (and most efficient) price of labour compared to what the market would have decided. The cult of equilibrium also suggests that unemployment simply signifies a person's unwillingness to sell their labour for a certain price. They choose not to work and go on holiday. The welfare state (including unemployment insurance and benefits) ruins these signals from the marketplace. And second, the notion of equilibrium (albeit with modifications by John Nash in non-cooperative situations) propagates the fable that capitalism is essentially a harmonious system, despite a few hiccups here and there. It elides the fact that capitalism is inherently extreme, crisis-ridden and dysfunctional, incapable of achieving any proper balance. The concept of equilibrium therefore presents a highly misleading picture of the economic system. Hence why economists considered the potato market equipoised during the Irish Famine... despite people starving.

Fiscal Constraint /ˈfɪsk(ə)l/ /kənˈstreɪnt/

The systematic reduction of public spending; a useless governmental tool for correcting the effects of the 2008 financial crisis.

Whereas the disaster of 2008 ought to have sunk neoliberal capitalism and spawned a host of civilised alternatives, governments and the corporate elite tried to save it by giving us an even more virulent strain of neoclassical economics. Stimulus packages and quantitative easing were a windfall to the banking sector, of course. But for everyone else, austerity has been hell. Public spending cuts were meant to jump-start business investment. Corporate tax relief was supposed to incentivise wage increases. And it was believed that low interest rates might spark lending. None of this happened. Most corporations simply kept the extra cash and are now awash with the stuff. The reason why austerity failed — even on its own terms — is because it had an unreal view of society. The economy is nothing like a household budget. As a result of fiscal constraint, the public sector is now anaemic and soon to die out.

Game Theory /ɡeɪm/ /ˈθɪəri/

The use of mathematics to model human reality; one of the more bizarre offshoots that followed the mathematisation of economic thought in the twentieth century.

Game theory focuses on strategies used by competing actors to make rational decisions. What should I do given my opponent may subsequently decide a, b, c or d? It was pioneered by John von Neumann, John Nash and Oskar Morgenstern. The assumption that social life is a game of logic between conniving actors is foundational to this view of economics. But do we really behave in such a "me vs. you" manner? Game Theory's rational individualism closely resonates with neoliberal capitalism because it reconceptualises everyone as mini-corporations who are totally selfish. Individuals compete rather than share; seek to outsmart the next person rather than empathise. Proponents of the approach often use the "as if" defence. The model might not perfectly match reality, but we can approximate how someone behaves in the real world by assuming they "act as" if they're Nashian plotters. It's the normative assumptions underlying this "as if" that are problematic… that at bottom we're all greedy and impatient bankers. One could just as well argue that people act "as if" they're trusting and altruistic socialists, but Game Theory won't have any of that.

Human Resource Management

/ˈhjuːmən/ /rɪˈsɔːs/ /ˈmanɪdʒm(ə)nt/

An ultra-corporate manifestation of business management; a practice informally called "Inhuman Resource Management" by workers.

Even the very phrase Human Resource Management (or HRM) sounds weird, like something dreamed up by extra-terrestrials who plan on harvesting mankind. The objectification is important to understanding HRM. In the old days, most large organisations had personnel departments. They dealt with payroll and hiring. In the 1980s and 1990s this role slowly focussed in on the nature of the employee. Testing potential recruits.

Developing employee engagement programmes to revive flagging morale and so on. However, the covert agenda was to replace unions, who had previously fulfilled these functions. As neoliberalism spread through the economy like wildfire, HRM became a tool for *pathologising* the recalcitrant employee. Rather than view the unhappy worker from a structural perspective (i.e., low wages, unfair treatment, boring job), it was their personality that was singled out as a problem. Following the financial crisis, HRM has become the punitive arm of organisational power. Their main role is to undermine unions, protect employers from discontented workers and enforce financial miserliness.

Informalism /ɪnˈfɔːm(ə)lɪz(ə)m/

Unregulated and spontaneous activity in the workplace; a zone of social interaction that has been transformed into an instrument of control by the modern corporation.

Neoliberalism hates formal organisations and especially bureaucracies. Bureaucracy is equated with red tape and government regulation, which clearly hinders free enterprise, according to the neoclassical doctrine. When it comes to workplace relations, there's been a concerted attempt to *deformalise* jobs and minimise statutory regulations and standards. Law (or lack thereof) has played an important part. Neoconservative legalists such as Richard Epstein have defended "at will contracts" where workers can be fired for any reason, with few statutory protections. The widespread use of arbitration waivers in the US echoes this trend too. Aggrieved employees must engage in private arbitration rather than participate in class actions. Uberisation also flirts with deformalisation since drivers, for example, aren't technically employees but ordinary citizens sharing a ride. The instrumentalisation of informality can be traced back to F.A. Hayek. He argued that economic actors should be free to do whatever they want behind closed doors. The state shouldn't interfere. The sentiment caught on. The Harvey Weinstein scandal gives us a flavour of what exactly can transpire behind those closed doors.

Key Performance Indicators /kiː/ /pəˈfɔːm(ə)ns/ /ˈɪndɪkeɪtəs/
The quantification of targets and work processes; a phrase that incites fear in most employees.
Metrics are now prominent in the corporate world and increasingly the public sector too. While management-by-objectives has been around for some time, it's the sheer level of quantification that makes Key Performance Indicators (or KPIs) unique. This avalanche of numbers is deemed to faithfully measure social behaviour. In light of big data and the return of authoritarian management, it was perhaps inevitable that KPIs would take on a rather tyrannical tenor. An undercover investigation of Amazon's head office by the *New York Times* revealed what happens when Big Data meets Big Brother. Almost every facet of office behaviour was numerically recorded and used to appraise workers. Stress, burnout and people crying at their desks were allegedly common occurrences. The problem with this approach to management is the "measure becomes the target" and the tail starts wagging the dog... as people sit crying at their desks.

Leadership /ˈliːdəʃɪp/

The assumption that when humans organise they require top-down control and only special individuals are capable of doing this; the valorisation of elitism.

When social actors are encouraged to behave as capsule-like monads — as they are under neoliberal capitalism — then some kind of extra-individual steering mechanism is soon required to avert chaos. In the workplace this could include workers' councils. At the societal level a democratically elected government. But capitalists naturally distain those options and evoke the mythology of leadership instead, sold to us as great men and women who've been blessed with amazing skills. To understand this bizarre veneration of elitism, we might recall Max Weber's argument about charismatic leaders. These individuals function as *supplements* to market rationality rather than replacements, which is why fascism was so attracted to the idea. The economic system can have bourgeois individualism and an overarching, CEO-like Führer at the same time. The conflation serves to ward off social democratic solutions to economic coordination.

"Lean In" /liːn/ /ɪn/

Faux-feminism for the corporate age; an attempt to render feminism business friendly; what feminism looks life after patriarchy wins.

Radical gender politics is dangerous to capitalism because it rallies against the patriarchal structures essential to it. In many ways, neoliberalism is a male-driven horror show. However, identity politics has severely diluted that radicalism and finally made feminism palatable to the establishment, including the multinational corporation. *Lean In: Women, Work and the Will to Lead*, by Sheryl Sandberg (Facebook's chief operating officer) is the end product of that betrayal. Sandberg gives advice to her readers about how to be both a woman and ruthlessly ambitious in the corporate world. Capitalism and the multinational corporation are all taken for granted, and feminism becomes a matter of women landing a seat in the boardroom and getting rich. This is the kind of "equality and diversity" that Theresa May and Gina Rinehart would happily support. Its message is "fit in" rather than challenge the system's flawed assumptions.

Moral Hazard /ˈmɒr(ə)l/ /ˈhazəd/

The cynical belief that you will automatically behave irresponsibly if not held accountable for your actions, especially in terms of financial responsibility; a moral pretext for demolishing the public sphere; the belief that everyone is a feckless opportunist.

The concept of moral hazard originated in insurance economics. It argues that once people are protected by insurance (say home and contents) they'll automatically engage in riskier behaviour than normal (leaving their homes unlocked, for example). The theory assumes that people are not only stupid but have no sense of civic responsibility. The rationale has been deployed by neocons to lay ruin to the welfare state. Unemployment insurance incentivises work avoidance. Public healthcare encourages unhealthy lifestyle choices, etc. We could follow the rationale *reductio ad absurdum*: public fire brigades shouldn't be funded because they inadvertently encourage people to be careless in the kitchen, and might result in them burning down their homes.

Networking /ˈnɛtwəːkɪŋ/

A bastardisation of social interaction under conditions of corporate hegemony; self-promotion; a ritual allowing the elite to distribute jobs among friends and family.

Instrumental, contrived and artificial, most who participate in networking events realise that something is profoundly wrong. Serial networkers tend to be inadequate in private, often hiding some terrible secret. Corporations once provided alcohol at these meetings — to oil the wheels of social interaction — until they discovered the booze was being used by networkers to numb their shame. Philosopher Gilles Deleuze might have been the earliest critic of this brutalised version of sociality: "Encounters with people are always catastrophic".

New Public Management /njuː/ /ˈpʌblɪk/ /ˈmanɪdʒm(ə)nt/

A trend in which public sector organisations adopt the management practices of private, for-profit businesses; an area of managerialism that stems from neoliberalism's loathing of the state.

New Public Management recommends that hospitals, the police force, universities, transportation agencies and childcare centres should take on the arcane language of corporations. Whereas public universities, for example, are supposed to be charities charged with a public mission, New Public Management encourages them to act like competitive businesses. All of a sudden students are customers. Lecturers become replaceable (and expendable) "employees" who must be micromanaged. In hospitals that have been neoliberalised, insuperable budget targets and KPIs are rampant. Advocates of New Public Management believe it makes government institutions more efficient and accountable. But public sector organisations don't work in the same way as private firms. For example, someone's motivation for becoming a nurse is different to a banker. The top-down control, lack of consultation and deep commercialisation that accompanies New Public Management demoralises the workforce. Ironically, supporters of this management approach often hold such a caricatured idea of what it means to be "corporate" that not even Goldman Sachs would recognise it.

Office Email /ˈɒfɪs/ /ˈiːmeɪl/

An electronic communication system that has become ubiquitous among the modern workforce; an instrument for spreading wage-theft and unpaid overtime; something 50% of the workforce now "check" outside of office hours.

What is colloquially called the "tranny of email", started life as a cool invention by Ray Tomlinson in 1971. With the birth of the Internet, email rapidly replaced memos and postage. In the workplace, it was meant to make life easier. However, smartphones turned this tool of convenience into a slave master, since the office is always there, in your pocket. Not so long ago management consultant's used to say they loved flying because only then could they turn off their phone. Now even that respite has disappeared, as WiFi coverage is included in most methods of travel. Email fits so snuggly into the neoliberal order because it exemplifies individual mobility. Like *homo economicus,* you're always switched on no matter what. Work and life merge. Self-exploitation becomes rife. But does email improve your productivity on the job? One study decided to find out. A large office was deprived of email access for a day and its productivity levels actually soared. Therefore, not only does the "tyranny of email" increase our workload and render us permanently exposed to the supervisor's gaze, it also hinders our ability to get things done, making life harder for no obvious reason.

Privatisation /prʌɪvətʌɪˈzeɪʃ(ə)n/

The erroneous belief that privately-owned enterprises manage services better than public ones; a euphemism for the transfer of wealth from the public sector to big business; the rise of parasitical outsourcing companies like G4S and Capita.

Liberalism has always favoured the private individual over government. Neoclassical economics extends the idea to the economy and corporations. The question is no longer framed as a moral issue ("we must protect private citizens from the state") but an economic one ("businesses are more efficient than public institutions"). This spurious idea has justified the sale of state assets, often at bargain-bin prices to large multinational firms. In many cases (as with transport, water, energy, etc.) these organisations remain monopolies, effectively making them *private governments,* facing little competition or public accountability. Owners are usually institutional investors located offshore who're only interested in the next dividend — privatisation is closely linked to the insanity of shareholder capitalism. The sale of state assets — and the outsourcing of services to private contractors — has been a social tragedy in most Western countries. It is incredible that some continue to beat the drum of privatisation in light of the cultural wastelands that London, Toronto, Auckland and New York have become, cities literally privatised to death. Privatisation is also an ethos. Individuals must internalise and live silently with the contradictions of capitalism alone. Hence the epidemic of depression and mental illness in many neoliberal countries.

Public Choice Theory /ˈpʌblɪk/ /tʃɔɪs/ /ˈθɪəri/

A conservative area of public economics that views the state not as neutral or impartial but as harbouring self-serving objectives; political science through the lens of neoclassical economics.

A leading theorist in this area, James M. Buchanan, said that he aimed to deromanticise government. For him, state officials engage in selfish "rent-seeking" behaviour and gain an unfair advantage over more competitive private enterprises. Buchanan explained budget deficits in the same manner:

> A politician who's seeking office or seeking to remain in office is responsible, as he should be, to constituents. He wants to go back to a constituency and tell them that he's either lowered their taxes, or he's brought them program benefits. You plug that into politics and you have a natural proclivity of a politician to create deficits.

As a result, democratic governments cannot be trusted with issues pertaining to the economy. That should be left to market forces and profit-maximising firms. It is telling that Buchanan frequently opts for the term "political process" over democracy. In this way Public Choice Theory is an important feature of the neoliberal arsenal for de-democratising Western societies.

Rational Choice Theory /ˈraʃ(ə)n(ə)l/ /tʃɔɪs/ /ˈθɪəri/
The myth of rational economic man; a model of individuals that views them as walking profit-and-loss calculators who think of nothing else.
Rational Choice Theory is fundamental to neoclassical economics and has helped spread the credo of *homo economicus* in many countries. The argument goes like this. People are motivated by utility-maximising behaviour. Utilities (or "utils") are quantifiable representations of things we want more of (satisfaction, benefits, pleasures, happiness, etc.). We rank these preferences and then rationally plan accordingly within the constraints of scarce resources (e.g., income, opportunity, etc.). Macroeconomists find the idea attractive because this activity can be mathematically modelled — such as $u(x1, x2; r1)=(x1 - r1) \alpha x2 \beta$. The US's fascination with Rational Choice Theory derives from its rebranding of citizens first as human capitalists and then as prudent consumers during the 1980s. An important implication of this theory is the sanctification of personal responsibility, which tacitly shifts capitalism's dysfunctions onto the individual. So,

you're unemployed? Then *you* must have made some bad decisions. There is nothing rational about Rational Choice Theory. In the words of Lorde, we are not a spreadsheet with hair.

Self-Management /sɛlf/ /ˈmanɪdʒm(ə)nt/

Worker discretion over their roles; the practice of doing your job and your boss's at the same time; self-exploitation.

Perhaps no other demand from the workers movement has been so exploited by the neoliberal enterprise. From the early years of industrialism up to the mid-1960s most jobs were managed by top-down hierarchies. Don't think, just follow orders. In the 1980s things changed. Employers realised that firms can squeeze more time/effort out of the workforce if they're given some responsibility over their jobs. Self-managing teams and empowerment were mainly about transferring the role of middle-managers onto the employee. What followed was an era of self-exploitation on a scale never before seen, which continues today. Workers' demand for democratic self-governance was transformed into the ultimate tool of self-control. As a result, the work day has extended because the division between work and private life breaks down under self-management. We become our jobs. The economy infiltrates the life process itself — just as neoclassical economic theory intended.

Shareholder Capitalism /ˈʃɛːhəʊldə/ /ˈkapɪt(ə)lɪz(ə)m/

Joint-stock and publically listed companies; a way that large corporations 'eat themselves'; one of the more ruthless forms of profiteering; according to former General Electric CEO, 'the worlds dumbest idea'.

Joint stock companies have been around for hundreds of years. Issuing shares is a way of generating greater levels of investment. However, today shareholder capitalism has become a sort of Frankenstein's monster and is wreaking havoc. When state assets in the transport, energy, water and telecommunications sectors were privatised in the 1980s, neoliberal politicians pitched it to the public as a chance for everyone to own part of these companies. That the public were technically *already* owners didn't seem to register. In reality most of the stock was purchased by large institutional investors, driven purely by short-term dividend gains. As a result, CEOs will do anything to raise the share price, which is often harmful to the long-term viability of the organisation and its surrounding environment. As an economist for the Bank of England put it, these corporations end up "eating themselves". With most profits being paid out as dividends to off-shore entities, reinvestment stalls and firms (including their workforce) are run into the ground, since that's counted as a "plus" on the next quarterly report. CEOs are given stock options to get them on board and then they too adopt a near suicidal short-term mindset, making millions in the process. The UK typifies the madness of shareholder capitalism. Its rail system and water service are dilapidated and falling apart, yet still happily charge customers extortionate prices. Bizarrely, some of these major investors are other governments, such as Germany and France, who then subsidise their own public infrastructure using profits made in the UK.

Tax Avoidance /taks/ /əˈvɔɪd(ə)ns/

How corporations and rich plutocrats sidestep the taxes that you and I have to pay; a mechanism for increasing wealth inequality to levels unheard of in the modern era; a method for starving the public sphere of cash; what greed looks like in the end times.

Neoliberalism has always hated tax, especially corporate tax. Trickledown economics assumes that low taxes incentivise employers to hire more workers, invest and grow. Instead, firms usually keep the extra equity and get richer. Building on that sentiment, corporations have devised an elaborate international system to facilitate tax avoidance, with the help of countries like Ireland (the "Double Irish") and Holland (the "Dutch Sandwich"). Corporations are taxed on profits rather than revenue. They can therefore artificially reduce these profits by setting up a parent company in Ireland, for example, and then a subsidiary in, say the UK, which is charged steep licensing and administrative fees. This is how Google can enjoy yearly sales in the UK of £1.03bn yet post a pre-tax profit of £149m, with a tax bill of £36.4m. Some firms might even record a "loss" (despite heathy revenues), then use the "Double Irish" with a "Dutch Sandwich", and pay no tax whatsoever. Combined with shadow banking, transfer pricing, trade misinvoicing and tax havens, here we see where neoliberal capitalism is heading in the end times. The ultra rich — and their phalanx — floating above the state as the public sphere shrinks and society descends into disorder. Moreover, it is precisely here that neo-Feudal social structures make a comeback, linked to family oligarchies and their tremendous influence over governments, bypassing the democratic process.

Uber /ˈuːbə/

Self-employment controlled by platform business models; a method firms use to externalise the costs of employment; a tax-avoidance strategy.

Ironically, the rise of the so-called "gig" and "sharing" economy is the fullest expression of market individualism as theorised by F.A. Hayek in *The Road to Serfdom*. People should not be part of any collective social form (like an organisation or union) but instead operate as isolated agents in the marketplace. Independent contractors, freelancers and agency staff follow this template. The idea was boosted by digital platforms that regulate the unincorporated worker in an on-demand fashion. This has been a boon for corporate capitalists because they can have their cake and eat it too. *De facto* employees tied to the company on the one hand. Private individuals who bear all the costs of employment and who can be dismissed at any time on the other. The sharing economy? More like the *share... or else!* economy. The ideology of Uber (or Uberisation) is spreading, and could very well represent the future of work.

Xe Services /ksɛ/ /ˈsəːvɪsɛs/

Necrocapitalism in full bloom; the blending of war and business; one step closer to the necrolypse.

Xe Services was once known as Blackwater Worldwide, then Xe and now Academi. One can note the softening of the name overtime as controversy followed the firm. Blackwater pioneered the use of private contractors in classified war missions. The company won governmental contracts worth US$2 billion between 1997 and 2010. In 2006 a Blackwater sniper killed three guards working for the Iraq Media Network. In 2007 employees were involved in the Nisour Square massacre in which seventeen civilians were gunned down. Despite these atrocities, the Obama Administration awarded the firm a further $210 million in contracts in 2010. Coupled with the Blair/Bush regime's illegitimate invasion of Iraq, the involvement of mercenaries like Blackwater typifies the marketisation of death under neoliberal capitalism. Or in the words of former CEO, Erik Prince, "an efficient, privatised solution to sclerotic and wasteful government bureaucracy". An ex-mercenary explains the real logic behind these business-militaries: "their very lack of accountability is their main selling point; they offer plausible deniability and brute force to those too weak or squeamish to wage war". Corporations like Academi are symptomatic of a more macabre turn in modern statecraft.

N   O   T   E   S

INTRODUCTION: CIRCLING THE DRAIN

[1] Vohs, K., Mead, N. and Goode, M. (2006). "The Psychological Consequences of Money". *Science*. 314: 1154-1156.

CHAPTER ONE: MISFUTURES OF THE PRESENT

[1] Henley, J. (2018). "Sweden distributes 'be prepared for war' leaflet to all 4.8m homes". *Guardian*. Available at https://www.theguardian.com/world/2018/may/21/sweden-distributes-be-prepared-for-war-cyber-terror-attack-leaflet-to-every-home

[2] *World Wide Fund for Nature* (2016). *Living Planet Report*. Available at http://awsassets.panda.org/downloads/lpr_living_planet_report_2016.pdf

[3] Lachman, D. (2018). "A Crisis is Coming". *US News*. Available at https://www.usnews.com/opinion/economic-intelligence/articles/2018-02-14/us-economy-is-in-danger-of-overheating-and-exploding-into-financial-crisis

[4] Basham, B. (2011). "Beware corporate psychopaths — they are still occupying positions of power". *Independent*. Available at https://www.independent.co.uk/news/business/comment/brian-basham-beware-corporate-psychopaths-they-are-still-occupying-positions-of-power-6282502.html

[5] Ellis, B.E. (1991). *American Psycho*. Picador: New York, p. 362.

[6] UBS/PwC. (2017). "Billionaires Report: New Value creators Gain Momentum". Available at https://www.ubs.com/microsites/billionaires-report/en/new-value.html

[7] O'Connell, M. (2018). "Why Silicon Valley billionaires are prepping for the apocalypse in New Zealand". *Guardian*. Available at https://www.theguardian.com/news/2018/feb/15/why-silicon-valley-billionaires-are-prepping-for-the-apocalypse-in-new-zealand

[8] McAndrew, F. (2015). "What Makes a House Feel Haunted?" *Psychology Today*. Available at https://www.psychologytoday.com/au/blog/out-the-ooze/201511/what-makes-house-feel-haunted

[9] Stuckler, D. Basu, S. (2013). *The Body Economic: Why Austerity Kills*. New York: Basic Books.

[10] Derrida, J. (1993). *Spectres of Marx: The State of the Debt, the Work of Mourning and the New International*. New York: Routledge.

[11] Ibid, p. 29.

[12] Fisher, M. (2014). *Ghosts of My Life: Writings on Depression, Hauntology and Lost Futures*. London: Zero0 Books.

[13] *Stop Autonomous Weapons* (2017). "Slaughterbots". Available at https://www.youtube.com/watch?v=9CO6M2HsoIA

[14] Pilkington, E. (2015). "Life as a drone operator: 'Ever step on ants and never give it another thought?'" *Guardian*. Available at https://www.theguardian.com/world/2015/nov/18/life-as-a-drone-pilot-creech-air-force-base-nevada

CHAPTER TWO: OPTIMISM IN THE DRONE AGE

[1] Sebald, W.G. (2003). *The Rings of Saturn*. New York: Vintage, pp. 78-79.

[2] Mathews, D. and Beauchamp, Z. (2016). "The UN library announced its most-checked-out book of 2015. It's kind of disturbing." *Vox*. Available at https://www.vox.com/2016/1/6/10724560/un-library-war-crimes

[3] Ibid.

[4] Sebald, W.G. (2001). "Books: Outside the Box — Interview with Malcom Jones." *Newsweek*. Available at https://www.newsweek.com/books-outside-box-153935

[5] Sebald, *The Rings of Saturn*, pp. 23-24.

[6] Chumley, C. (2013). "Obama brags, in new book: I'm 'really good at killing people' with drones". *Washington Times*. Available at https://www.washingtontimes.com/news/2013/nov/4/obama-brag-new-book-im-really-good-killing-drones/

[7] *American Civil Liberties Union* (2018). "Targeted Killing". Available at https://www.aclu.org/issues/national-security/targeted-killing

[8] Chumley, "Obama brags, in new book: I'm 'really good at killing people' with drones".

[9] *Channel Four Despatches* (2018). "Inside Facebook: Secrets of a Social Network". Available at https://www.channel4.com/programmes/inside-facebook-secrets-of-a-social-network

[10] Wiedeman, R. (2018). "The Company Built on a Bluff". *New York Magazine.* Available at http://nymag.com/daily/intelligencer/2018/06/inside-vice-media-shane-smith.html

[11] Pinker, S. (2011). *The Better Angles of Our Nature: Why Violence Has Declined.* New York: Viking Books.

[12] Ibid, p. xxv.

[13] Pinker, S. (2018). *Enlightenment Now: The Case for Reason, Science, Humanism, and Progress.* New York: Viking.

[14] Ibid, p. 49.

[15] Acquilla, J. (2012). "The Big Kill". *Foreign Policy.* Available at https://foreignpolicy.com/2012/12/03/the-big-kill/

[16] Peterson, J. (2018). "Jordan Peterson talks Lobsters on Channel 4". Available at https://www.youtube.com/watch?v=bZnygvRRmPE

[17] Dorling, D. (2018). *Do We Need Economic Inequality?* Cambridge: Polity Press.

[18] Ibid, p. 113.

[19] Sebald, *The Rings of Saturn*, pp. 78-79.

CHAPTER THREE: IS CAPITALISM A CULT?

[1] Reeves, A. McKee, M. and Stuckler, D. (2014). "Economic Suicides in the Great Recession in Europe and North America". *British Journal of Psychiatry*. 20(3): pp. 246-247.

[2] Blyth, M. (2013). *Austerity: The History of a Dangerous Idea*. New York: University of Oxford Press, p. 229.

[3] Becker, G. (2010). "Gary Becker — The Economist's Economist". *Hoover Institution*. Available at https://www.youtube.com/watch?v=QT6TnY6sHcU

[4] Festinger, L. Riecken, H. and Schachter, S. (1956). *When Prophecy Fails*. New York: Harper.

[5] *Cultwatch* (2018). "How to leave and recover from a Religious Cult". Available at https://www.cultwatch.com/how-to-leave-recover.html

CHAPTER FOUR: SHITTY ROBOTS

[1] *CNBC* (2016). "Hot Robot At SXSW Says She Wants To Destroy Humans". Available at https://www.youtube.com/watch?v=W0_DPi0PmF0

[2] Wong, V. (2018). Amazon Knows Alexa Devices Are Laughing Spontaneously And It's 'Working To Fix It'". *BuzzFeed.* Available at https://www.buzzfeed.com/venessawong/amazon-alexa-devices-are-laughing-creepy?utm_term=.xlPpPQPyB#.ut7eLQLjV

[3] Gander, K. (2015). Worker Killed by Robot at Volkswagen Car Factory". *Independent.* Available at https://www.independent.co.uk/news/world/europe/worker-killed-by-robot-at-volkswagen-car-factory-10359557.html

[4] Davies, W. (2015). "Silly robots!" *Chronicle of Higher Education.* Available at http://chronicle.com/article/Silly-Robots-/233965

[5] Wakefield, J. (2018). "Are you scared yet? Meet Norman, the psychopathic AI". *BBC.* Available at https://www.bbc.com/news/technology-44040008

[6] Less Wrong (2017). "Paperclip Maximizer". Available at https://wiki.lesswrong.com/wiki/Paperclip_maximizer

[7] Yudkowsky, E. (2008). "Artificial Intelligence as a Positive and Negative Factor in Global Risk". In *Global Catastrophic Risks*, edited by Nick Bostrom and Milan M.Čirković, New York: Oxford University Press, pp. 308–345

[8] Greenhouse, S. (2016). "Autonomous vehicles could cost America 5 million jobs. What should we do about it?" *LA Times*. Available at: http://www.latimes.com/opinion/op-ed/la-oe-greenhouse-driverless-job-loss-20160922-snap-story.html

[9] Brynjolfsson, E. and McAfee, A. (2014). *The Second Machine Age: Work, Progress, and Prosperity in a Time of Brilliant Technologies*. New York: Norton.

[10] Sherwood, H. (2017). "Robot Priest Unveiled in Germany to Mark 500 Years Since Reformation". *Guardian*. Available at https://www.theguardian.com/technology/2017/may/30/robot-priest-blessu-2-germany-reformation-exhibition

[11] Andrews, T. (2016). "Meet the Robot Monk Spreading the Teachings of Buddhism Around China". *Washington Post*. Available at: https://www.washingtonpost.com/news/morning-mix/wp/2016/04/27/meet-the-robot-monk-spreading-the-teachings-of-buddhism-around-china/?utm_term=.5b6fdca8498a

[12] Miller, D. (2012). "Think You've Got a Bad Job? Indian 'Sewer Diver' Paid Just £3.50 a Day (Plus a Bottle of Booze) to Unclog Delhi's Drains". *Daily Mail*. Available at: http://www.dailymail.co.uk/news/article-2190251/And-thought-bad-job-Indian-sewer-diver-paid-just-3-50-day-plus-bottle-booze-unclog-Delhis-drains.html

[13] Limaye, Y. (2016). "India's Sewer Workers Risking Their Lives". *BBC*. Available at: http://www.bbc.co.uk/news/business-35958730

[14] Booth, R. (2016). "More Than 7m Britons Now in Precarious Employment". *Guardian*. Available at: https://www.theguardian.com/uk-news/2016/nov/15/more-than-7m-britons-in-precarious-employment

[15] *Resolution Foundation* (2015). "26 percentage point gap between best and worst parts of the UK for BAME employment". Available at: http://www.resolutionfoundation.org/media/press-releases/26-percentage-point-gap-between-best-and-worst-parts-of-the-uk-for-bame-employment/

[16] *US Bureau of Labor Statistics* (2016). "A Profile of the Working Poor". Available at: https://www.bls.gov/opub/reports/working-poor/2014/pdf/home.pdf

[17] Silver, B. (2003). *Forces of Labor: Workers' Movements and Globalization Since 1870*. New York: Cambridge University Press.

[18] *Maritime Union of Australia* (2014). "Industry Wises Up to Automation". Available at: http://www.mua.org.au/industry_wises_up_to_automation

[19] Saulwick, J. (2015). "Sydney's Patrick Terminal Goes Automated, With Fewer Staff but Dancing Robots". *Sydney Morning Herald*. Available at: http://www.smh.com.au/nsw/sydneys-patrick-terminal-goes-automated-with-fewer-staff-but-dancing-robots-20150617-ghqc24.html

[20] Scott, A. (2017). "Boeing Studies Pilotless Planes as It Ponders Next Jetliner". *Reuters*. Available at http://www.reuters.com/article/us-boeing-airshow-autonomous-idUSKBN18Z12M

[21] Reiner, A. (2016). "Towards the End of Pilots". *Atlantic*. Available at: https://www.theatlantic.com/technology/archive/2016/03/has-the-self-flying-plane-arrived/472005/

[22] Savage, M. (2015). *Social Class in the 21st Century*. London: Penguin.

[23] Buranyi, S. (2018). "Dehumanising, Impenetrable, Frustrating: the Grim Reality of Job Hunting in the Age of AI". *Guardian*. Available at https://www.theguardian.com/inequality/2018/mar/04/dehumanising-impenetrable-frustrating-the-grim-reality-of-job-hunting-in-the-age-of-ai.

[24] See Eubanks, V. (2018). *Automating Inequality: How High-Tech Tools Profile, Police, and Punish the Poor*. New York: Macmillan.

CHAPTER FIVE: OFFICE HATESCAPES

[1] Walford, J. (2018). "University Tutor Died after 'Silently Struggling' with Workload". *Wales Online*. Available at https://www.walesonline.co.uk/news/wales-news/university-tutor-died-after-silently-14751533

[2] *BBC* (2019)."France Telecom Suicides: Former Bosses Face Trial". Available at https://www.bbc.com/news/world-europe-44507597

[3] Hirigoyen, M. (2018). "Moral Harassment". *Prevent Violence at Work*. Available at http://www.prevention-violence.com/en/int-111.asp

[4] Ryall, J. (2018). "Quarter of Japanese Workers Confess They Want to Kill Their Boss". *Telegraph*. Available at https://www.telegraph.co.uk/news/2018/06/22/quarter-japanese-workers-confess-want-kill-boss/

[5] Keltner, D. (2016). *The Power Paradox*. New York: Penguin,

[6] Keltner, D. (2016). "Don't Let Power Corrupt You". *Harvard Business Review*. October: pp. 112-115.

[7] Brooks, N, Fritzon, K and Croom, S. *(2016)*. "The Emergence of Noncriminal Psychopathy". Paper presented at the *Australian Psychological Society Conference*.

[8] Babiak, P. and Hare, R. (2007). *Snakes in Suits: When Psychopaths Go to Work*. New York: Harpers.

[9] See Graeber, D. (2015).*The Utopia of Rules: On Technology, Stupidity, and the Secret Joys of Bureaucracy*. New York: Melville House.

[10] Chung, F. (2018). "'You are really getting on my tits': Sydney boss slams lazy staff in brutal Friday email". *News.com.au*. Available at https://www.news.com.au/finance/work/at-work/you-are-really-getting-on-my-tits-sydney-boss-slams-lazy-staff-in-brutal-friday-email/news-story/62e729eddef16cda15e3e6e73d283c1b

[11] Moulds, J. (2018). "Robot Managers: The Future of Work or a Step Too Far?" *Guardian*. Available at https://www.theguardian.com/business-to-business/2018/apr/06/robot-managers-how-a-firm-automated

[12] Buranyi, S. (2018). "Dehumanising, Impenetrable, Frustrating: the Grim Reality of Job Hunting in the Age of AI". Guardian. Available at https://www.theguardian.com/inequality/2018/mar/04/dehumanising-impenetrable-frustrating-the-grimreality-of-job-hunting-in-the-age-of-ai.

[13] Marsh, L. (2018). "The Coping Economy". *Dissent*. Available at https://www.dissentmagazine.org/article/coping-economy-mindfulness-goes-corporate

[14] Rudd, J. (2017). "Long Working Days Can Cause Heart Problems, Study Says". *Guardian*. Available at https://www.theguardian.com/science/2017/jul/14/long-working-days-can-cause-heart-problems-study-says

[15] *Australia National University* (2017). "A Healthy Work Limit Is 39 Hours per Week". Available at http://www.anu.edu.au/news/all-news/a-healthy-work-limit-is-39-hours-per-week

[16] Hill, A. (2017). "There's a Danger of a Generation Who Can't Afford to Retire". *Guardian*. https://www.theguardian.com/membership/2017/jan/23/saving-retirement-pension-generation-old-age

CHAPTER SIX: THE PSYCHO-NANNY STATE

[1] *Department of Homeland Security* (2018). "DHS Secretary Nielsen's Remarks on the Illegal Immigration Crisis". Available at https://www.dhs.gov/news/2018/06/18/dhs-secretary-nielsens-remarks-illegal-immigration-crisis

[2] Smith, D. (2018). "Trump Administration Scrambles as Outrage Grows over Border Separations". *Guardian*. Available at https://www.theguardian.com/us-news/2018/jun/18/us-immigration-border-families-separated-children-kirstjen-nielsen

[3] Rosenberg, E. (2018). "Ann Coulter Tells Trump That Immigrant Children Are 'Child Actors', in Fox News Interview". *Independent*. Available at https://www.independent.co.uk/news/world/americas/us-politics/ann-coulter-fox-news-trump-immigrant-children-child-actors-zero-tolerance-policy-a8405631.html

[4] *Guardian* (2018). "'It's inhumane': the Windrush victims who have lost jobs, homes and loved ones". Available at https://www.theguardian.com/uk-news/2018/apr/20/its-inhumane-the-windrush-victims-who-have-lost-jobs-homes-and-loved-ones

[5] Ibid.

[6] Hughes, P. (2018). "Put on a Jamaican accent to avoid attention, British Government tells deportees". *I-News*. Available at https://inews.co.uk/news/politics/put-on-a-jamaican-accent-to-avoid-attention-british-government-tells-deportees/

[7] O'Connor, L. (2018). "President of American Academy of Paediatrics Calls Trump Border Policy 'Child Abuse.'" *Huffington Post*. Available at https://www.huffingtonpost.com.au/entry/pediatrics-academy-border-separation-child-abuse_us_5b27f437e4b0783ae12bfe6d

[8] Lippmann, W. (1925/1993). *The Phantom Public*. New York: Macmillan, p. 51.

[9] Meier, H. (1995). *Carl Schmitt and Leo Strauss: The Hidden Dialogue*. Chicago: University of Chicago Press, p. 125

[10] Lockhart, P. R. (2018). "Police shot and killed an unarmed black man in his own backyard. All he was holding was a cellphone". *Vox*. Available at https://www.vox.com/identities/2018/3/21/17149092/stephon-clark-police-shooting-sacramento

[11] *BBC* (2018). "Trump space force: US to set up sixth military branch". Available at https://www.bbc.com/news/world-us-canada-44527672

[12] *BBC* (2013). "Bain Capital buys stake in UK government blood company". Available at https://www.bbc.com/news/uk-politics-23372989

CHAPTER SEVEN: HELL WOULDN'T EVEN HAVE US

[1] Donnellan, A. (2018). "Animal Ear Tags among Plastic and Metal Rubbish Being Ground up and Put into Pet Food, Insiders Confirm". *Australian Broadcasting Corporation*. Available at http://www.abc.net.au/news/2018-06-19/pet-food-insider-lifts-lid-on-plastic-and-rubbish-going-into-pe/9875184

[2] *CNBC* (2009). "Male Chicks Ground up Alive at Egg Hatcheries". Available at http://www.cbc.ca/news/male-chicks-ground-up-alive-at-egg-hatcheries-1.823644

[3] Pachaud, L. (2017). "Working Undercover on a Factory Farm Traumatized Me". *Lilly*. Available at https://www.thelily.com/working-undercover-on-a-factory-farm-traumatized-me/

[4] Carlson, C. (2012). "Undercover Factory Farm Investigator Shares His Story". *Animals Australia*. Available at https://www.animalsaustralia.org/media/opinion.php?op=273

[5] Kolbert, E. (2014). *The Sixth Extinction: An Unnatural History.* New York: Picador.

[6] *World Wide Fund for Nature* (2016). "Living Planet Report". Available at http://awsassets.panda.org/downloads/lpr_living_planet_report_2016.pdf

[7] Bar-On, Y. Phillips, R. and Milo, M. (2017). "The Biomass Distribution on Earth". *Proceedings of the National Academy of Sciences*. Available at http://www.pnas.org/content/115/25/6506

[8] Hallmann, C., et al. (2017). "More than 75 Percent Decline over 27 Years in Total Flying Insect Biomass in Protected Areas". *Plos One*. Available at http://journals.plos.org/plosone/article?id=10.1371/journal.pone.0185809

[9] Jacobs, B. (2018). "Republican Congressman Explains Sea-Level Rise: It's Rocks Falling Into The Sea". *Huffington Post*. Available at https://www.huffingtonpost.com/entry/republican-congressman-explains-sea-level-rise-its-rocks-falling-into-the-sea_us_5afef746e4b07309e057985b

[10] Milman, O. (2014). "Tony Abbott Adviser Warns of Threat of Global Cooling". *Guardian*. Available at https://www.theguardian.com/environment/2014/aug/14/tony-abbott-adviser-warns-of-threat-of-global-cooling

[11] Klein, N. (2015). *This Changes Everything: Capitalism Vs. The Climate*. New York: Simon & Schuster; David, L. (2006). *Stop Global Warming: The Solution Is You!* New York: Fulcrum Publishing.

[12] Moore, J. (2015). *Capitalism in the Web of Life: Ecology and the Accumulation of Capital*. London: Verso.

[13] Kolbert, E. (2013). "The Lost World". *New Yorker*. Available at https://www.newyorker.com/magazine/2013/12/23/the-lost-world-3

[14] Jensen, D. (2006). *Endgame*. New York: Seven Stories Press.

[15] Ibid, p. 125.

CHAPTER EIGHT: DIGITAL-TO-DUST

[1] Ong, T. (2018). "Amazon patents wristbands that track warehouse employees' hands in real time". *Verge*. Available at https://www.theverge.com/2018/2/1/16958918/amazon-patents-trackable-wristband-warehouse-employees

[2] Byung-Chul, H. (2017). *Psychopolitics: Neoliberalism and New Technologies of Power*. London: Verso.

[3] Ibid, p. 36.

[4] Gray, J. (2014). *The Silence of Animals: On Progress and Other Modern Myths*. New York: Farrar Straus & Giroux

CONCLUSION: LOW

[1] Fisher, M. and Ambrose, D. (ed.). (2018). *k-punk: The Collected and Unpublished Writings of Mark Fisher (2004-2016)*. London: Repeater Books.

REPEATER BOOKS

is dedicated to the creation of a new reality. The landscape of twenty-first-century arts and letters is faded and inert, riven by fashionable cynicism, egotistical self-reference and a nostalgia for the recent past. Repeater intends to add its voice to those movements that wish to enter history and assert control over its currents, gathering together scattered and isolated voices with those who have already called for an escape from Capitalist Realism. Our desire is to publish in every sphere and genre, combining vigorous dissent and a pragmatic willingness to succeed where messianic abstraction and quiescent co-option have stalled: abstention is not an option: we are alive and we don't agree.

ACKNOWLEDGEMENTS

Tariq Goddard at Repeater Books started the ball rolling on this book. I thank him for his patience, insight and friendship. Josh Turner provided excellent editorial support and guidance. Needless to say, all mistakes and inaccuracies I alone am responsible for. This book wouldn't have happened if Amelia and Elliot hadn't kept the world intact. And special mention to my friends – present and past – in England and Europe… you know who you are.